Catskill Ghosts

Catskill Ghosts

History & Hauntings in the Catskill Mountain Region

Lynda Lee Macken

CATSKILL GHOSTS
History & Hauntings in the Catskill Mountain Region
Black Cat Press
P. O. Box 1218
Forked River, NJ 08731

ISBN 978-0-9829580-9-4

Book Layout & Cover Design by Deb Tremper, Six Penny Graphics.
www.sixpennygraphics.com

Printed in the United States of America by Sheridan Books, Inc.
www.sheridan.com

To Liv. Always.

Contents

Lake with Dead Trees (Catskill), 1825 by Thomas Cole

Introduction

"The whole neighborhood abounds with local tales, haunted spots, and twilight superstitions; stars shoot and meteors glare oftener across the valley."
—Washington Irving

The hauntingly beautiful Catskill Mountains possess a supernatural quality that renders the region a perfect setting for the paranormal. Without question, Washington Irving's "Rip Van Winkle" is the Catskill's most famous, *fictional* ghost story. Van Winkle slumbered in the highlands and awoke to realize twenty years passed, and so did the American Revolution. Penned in 1818, the narrative tells of Van Winkle's encounter with the ghosts of Henry Hudson's *Half Moon* crew who haunt Kaaterskill Falls.

Integral to the story, Irving called the highlands a "region full of fable," alluding to the many tales of strange happenings in the region. Irving wrote the mountain settlements were "subject to marvelous events and appearances." Did the author presage the plethora of hauntings prevalent today? The following stories corroborate Irving's "spellbound region" description for the territory flourishes with supernatural shenanigans.

Native Americans living in the mountains considered the peaks the abode of spirits. Tales of "spook woods" and "spook hollows" developed as settlers explored the diverse terrain comprised of tangled, dark forests filled with strange sounds.

Established as a trading post in 1614, Kingston existed as the Dutch colony originally called Wiltwyck. The city is home to some of the country's oldest homes, and the oldest public building—the original State Senate building, erected in 1676. Kingston bears the distinction of being New York's State's first capital and boasts several locations harboring a ghost or two.

Historic Huguenot Street, located in New Paltz, comprises seven stone houses built by Huguenot settlers who fled discrimination and religious persecution in the 17th century. Initially occupied by Native Americans, the Wallkill River site is one of the oldest continuously inhabited settlements in the United States. History and hauntings go hand in hand so it's no surprise many of the old dwellings house spirits. On July 3, 1878, *The New York Times* proclaimed Ulster County a hotbed of paranormal activity stating the county seems to be "a favored neighborhood for ghostly visitations and other things of a marvelous nature."

Roughly translated, "Schoharie" is the Iroquois word for "to cross over." Clearly, the spirits who haunt the Schoharie County Old Stone Fort Museum (1752) have yet to transition to the other side. The role patriots played in our nation's history continues to echo through time. Another county specter is Grace Stacey who exerts her post-mortem influence at Cobleskill's 1802 Bull's Head Inn.

The Catskills possess a history of homicides like Sally Hamilton, a 20-year old Athens woman. In 1813, her slain body surfaced in a local brook, now dubbed "Murderers' Creek." Near Leeds, the ghost of a young servant girl, Anna Dorothea Swarts, still haunts. She died at the hands of her master who attempted to corral her rebellious spirit.

Starting in 1825, Thomas Cole, and other painters of the Hudson River School, attracted people to the mountains with their beautiful landscape paintings. Cole, considered the father of the art movement, lived in the town of Catskill where his spirit is still discerned.

Apparitions are the rarest of all paranormal phenomena. Spirit manifestations can be the result of imprinted energy fields rooted in some intensely traumatic incident occurring at a location. Hence the sightings at Kenoza Lake's Stone Arch Bridge where George Markert took his last breath in 1892.

The Catskill Mountain region once personified excitement and allure for East Coast, middle-class families. Known as the "Borscht Belt," upstate hotels drew mostly Jewish guests who were often unwelcome at other lodgings. At its heyday in the 1960s, the swanky nightclubs offered big-name entertainment, such as musicians Louis Armstrong, Duke Ellington, and Dean Martin, and comics Rodney Dangerfield, Jerry Lewis, and Joan Rivers, to name a few.

For those unfamiliar with the "Jewish Alps," the movie *Dirty Dancing* offers an accurate depiction. The movie, written and co-produced by Eleanor Bergstein, is based on the author's experiences at Grossinger's Catskill Resort Hotel, the place where she summered as a young woman. *Dirty Dancing* typifies life at the all-inclusive vacation hotels. This period also makes it mark in the spirits left behind.

The town of Woodstock is America's oldest and most successful art colony. The infamous Woodstock music festival held at nearby Yasgur's dairy farm in August 1969, attracted nearly half a million people, and will forever keep Woodstock on the map. While recording at the Bearsville Studios, legendary performer Meat Loaf underwent an eerie encounter that haunted him for decades.

All that ever existed, exists eternally yet change is inevitable. Time marches on, sometimes leaving ethereal traces of the past in its wake; unearthly residues endure and exude a special lure to the Catskill Mountains locale.

Our perennial fascination with the unknown, combined with the desire to believe life carries on, albeit in another dimension, ensures the spirits who haunt the Catskills of New York State will not be forgotten. I am pleased to chronicle these haunting tales and help enliven the region's storied landmarks with *spirit*.

"What the Catskills lack in vastness they make up in mystery, the mystery of dark forests and caverns, of unexpected grassy meadows, innumerable paths and roads that lead nowhere, hidden springs and cascades, for the Catskills specialize in cascades. The spots devoid of trees are not flat granite rocks like the Adirondacks—the rocks of the Catskills have a tendency toward the artistic; mosses, ferns, fallen trees, acres of tangled laurel fill up the gaps, and the white birch springs up quickly and adds beauty and ghostliness."
—J. VanVechten Veeder, *Historic Catskill*

Murderers' Creek, Athens

Murderers' Creek

The archetypal "woman in white" is a classic female ghost reportedly seen in rural areas and associated with some tragic local legend. Stories of "white ladies" appear all over the world, most often related to the restless spirit of a woman who died a violent death. She haunts cemeteries, country lanes, or in this case, Murderers' Creek.

Murderers' Creek joins the Hudson River to Sleepy Hollow Lake north of the town of Athens. The first reference to the name "Murderer's Kill" is from a 1673 land deed. Most likely the name derived from the Dutch pronunciation of "Mother's Creek," *moeder* and *kille*. In the early 19th century, the slain body of Sally Hamilton surfaced in the stream. Local legend says the creek's modern name originated from this event.

On the evening of August 25, 1813, Sally Hamilton left her sister Lucy's house and headed to her parents' home about a half-mile away. The friends who accompanied Sally wanted to go shopping but she declined, feeling eager to get home. Sally continued on her way and encountered two elderly women. She walked with them for a while and parted ways close to her house. That was the last time Sally was seen alive.

A local newspaper describing Sally stated she was "of a very respectable family, and possessed to the full an equal share of the attractions and accomplishments of her sex; superadded to which, she enjoyed a most irreproachable character." When the 20-year-old disappeared, alarm sounded and the entire town set out to find the missing woman. A couple of local residents thought they heard a woman in distress but authorities dismissed their statements.

Three days later, Sally's body surfaced in the creek, a half mile north of the bridge. Her body showed evidence of a struggle and blunt force trauma which killed her. Her assailant(s) was never apprehended.

Sadly, almost thirty years later, another unspeakable homicide occurred. George Eliot murdered Mary Johnson in 1841 and buried her under the creek bridge.

The spirits of both Sally Hamilton and Mary Johnson haunt Murderers' Creek. Some specters of those who died suddenly or unexpectedly remain confused either not knowing or accepting they are dead. They stay earthbound trying to connect with passersby, who might be sensitive to spirits, hoping they can help them understand their plight.

Substance beyond this material universe appears translucent which describes the women-in-white wandering the environs of Murderers' Creek. Countless witnesses offer accounts of the murdered women's apparitions. Not all find the experience frightful—some actually consider the manifestation comforting and transformative.

Do the murdered women's spirits still rise from Murderers' Creek on mist-laden mornings or take flight in the dark of night? Plan a visit to this reputedly haunted place and discover for yourself.

What is a "kill?"

A "kill" is a body of water, most commonly a creek, but also a tidal inlet, river or straight. The term derives from the Middle Dutch *kille*, meaning "riverbed" or "water channel." "Kill" frequently appears in place names of the region, such as Bear Kill, Catskill, Cobleskill, Fantinekill, Kaaterskill, Leurenkill, Murderers' Kill and Wallkill, among others.

Stewart House

2 North Water Street
Athens

The Village of Athens sits on the Hudson River, four miles north of the Rip Van Winkle Bridge in Greene County. First settled in the late 17th century, the village, a port for the Hudson-Athens Ferry, became a thriving hub for shipbuilding, brick making, and ice harvesting. When the bridge opened in 1935, the ferry became obsolete and closed in 1947.

Athens remains substantially unchanged since its heyday in the late 19th century. The village enjoys more than 300 buildings on national and state historic registers and is virtually a living museum of American design boasting many architectural styles, among them Victorian, Georgian and Federal.

Back in the day, impromptu steamboat races commonly occurred on the Hudson; the rationale being the fastest boat would attract the most passengers. Officially illegal, the practice caused awful accidents including the most famous Hudson River shipwreck, the steamboat *Swallow*.

Built in New York City in 1836, the steamer navigated the nighttime run between Manhattan and Albany. Her 426-ton weight did not deter her speed. Along with the steamship Rochester, they were known as "Hudson River Flyers" and often raced one another.

One of the most famous Hudson River shipwrecks is the steamboat *Swallow*. Built in New York City in 1836, the steamer navigated the nighttime run between Manhattan and Albany. Her wooden hull measured as long as a football field and her 426 ton weight did not deter her speed. Along with the steamship *Rochester*, they were known as "Hudson River Flyers" and often raced one another.

On April 7, 1845, the *Swallow*, captained by A.H. Squires, left Albany for New York City with over 300 passengers. The *Rochester*, commanded by Captain Crittenden and another side-wheeler called the *Express*, soon followed. Most of the passengers were unaware of the ensuing race.

That night, a heavy gale prevailed with scattered snow squalls. As the *Swallow* neared Athens, the pilot lost his bearings in the blinding storm and the boat crashed onto

Dooper's Island, a rocky outcropping near the shore. The earsplitting collision shattered the hull and the ship burst into flames. The *Swallow* quickly sank.

Do some of the drowning victims' spirits haunt the Stewart House? Some speculate they do.

A few of the passengers made it safely to land; many jumped into the river but became disoriented in the dark. Church bells tolled and hundreds of Athens' citizenry quickly responded, some stoked fires to provide light and many sought to save as many people as possible. Other boats, along with smaller crafts, rescued about 300 people. At least 40 perished, although the exact number of fatalities is unknown due to non-existent passenger records.

Restored and renovated to showcase the structure's period detail, wood moldings, panels, floors, and spindles are some of the unique details creating a timeless atmosphere. A backward "S" appears on a large iron plate outside the Stewart's southeast entrance. Perhaps the person who molded this decorative finishing touch made a mistake and the error not considered important enough to change. Maybe the backward S indicated a bold fashion statement. This curious novelty is not the only anomaly at this piece of history. One of the strangest oddities is the mystery of the keys.

Some staffers and guests hear the sound of keys jangling in the corridors. Not the rattling of a modern keychain but the noise of heavy keys banging together on an old-fashioned ring. Most often, the sound is discerned late at night when it's suggested Hardy Stewart's spirit goes about locking the inn. Refurbished to reflect much of its original appearance, the long-gone innkeeper's spirit undoubtedly feels right at home. Room keys often go missing as well but eventually surface days later in the most improbable places.

Other spooky phenomena include the inexplicable opening and closing of doors. Incorporeal footsteps and faint voices echo throughout the hallways.

In *Ghost Investigator, Back into the Light*, author Linda Zimmerman told the story of an employee who witnessed containers flying off a shelf in the hotel's storage room. The invisible entity seemed to forcefully sweep the items off the shelf. Speaking of sweeping, one chef observed a broom moving on its own as if the disembodied spirit performed its chores!

The benign spirits who roam the Stewart House add a haunting chapter to the lodge's storied legacy. Most believe the reason these souls stay behind is to continue watching over the establishment, taking care to ensure the patrons a quality experience.

Minisink Battleground

County Route 168
Barryville

During the American Revolution, the Catskills served as buffer between British Canada and New York City. In the summer of 1779, Mohawk chief Joseph Brant led a raiding party of about 80 Indians and American British sympathizers known as Tories in raids along the Delaware Valley. The Battle of Minisink became one of the deadliest Revolutionary War encounters for the Colonial side.

On July 22, 1779, Colonel John Hathorn and more than 100 soldiers pursued Brant into the Upper Delaware wildernesses. The forces met at present day Minisink Ford, where a failed ambush led Brant to declare victory after the slaughter of 46 militia men during a day-long battle. Most of the dead lay exposed on the field for *43 years*, until a mass burial in Barryville's Congregational Church graveyard, and later to Goshen, took place.

Minisink Battleground Park conducts an annual commemoration to honor the patriots who perished here defending liberty. Colonial re-enactors invigorate the living history demonstrations honoring the day. Many report unusual feelings and experiences while visiting the battleground park.

"Orb photo taken at Hospital Rock, the rock outcropping on the Minisink Battleground where Lt. Colonel Benjamin Tusten, a medical doctor, treated the wounds of his fellow militiamen when they were all killed by Joseph Brant's men." Photo courtesy of John Conway.

John Conway, Sullivan County historian, disclosed that during one of the memorial ceremonies, a guest speaker sighted apparitions of three men. Each of the specters wore colonial garb and brandished colonial era muskets. The trio stood in a corner of the field talking to one another. The guest speaker clearly heard one of them referred to as "Knapp," and wondered if he fought or died in the battle. (According to Conway, two men named Knapp, Samuel and James, perished during the conflict). The speaker also discerned one of the men express his eagerness to get home to his pregnant wife.

The speaker, who wishes to remain anonymous, went on to reveal to Conway that he underwent an out-of-body experience during a medical procedure years earlier. Since that occasion, he gained a heightened psychic sense that manifests as visions and intuitions.

Residential houses exist nearby the battleground. When a young boy arrived home, his mother asked what he had been doing. *"Playing with a soldier,"* he replied. Much to his mother's consternation, the youth went on to describe a colonial-era combatant. Is this one of the same spirits sighted by the guest speaker?

This sad story of an earthbound spirit is one of thousands. Around the globe, ghosts continue to haunt the places where they fell during war. A battle need not be major to instigate ghosts of war. Some of the men who died during the Minisink battle left behind their families. Perhaps this unknown soldier's spirit is comforted by playing with a youngster, maybe thinking of his own son at home.

Spirits remain stuck between our earthly dimension and the spirit world for any number of reasons. For instance, they reject the concept of an afterlife, don't realize they're dead, or cannot accept their death. Maybe the soldiers' spirits appear and reach out to the living in hope they can be helped. Spirit rescuers assist spirit entities to transition into the afterlife—assistance much needed at this site and battlefields all over the world.

"It is up to the living to help ghosts, to acknowledge them, so they can accept their reality, gain peace and move on."
—David J. Pitkin

Bearsville Residence

The town of Woodstock originated as a Dutch settlement and became America's oldest and most successful art colony. The woods, farmland, lakes and Hudson River views, and the area's proximity to New York City, motivated Ralph Radcliffe Whitehead and his wife, Jane Byrd McCall, to purchase fifteen hundred acres on Mount Guardian.

In 1902, the pair created a utopian art colony they called Byrdcliffe. Artists, writers, musicians, social reformers and intellectuals came from across the country to gain inspiration from nature and like-minded people. Bob Dylan lived in a house at Byrdcliffe in the '60s and early '70s. The colony eventually expanded into outlying Bearsville.

Manager/producer Albert Grossman founded Bearsville Records in 1969. For decades his Bearsville Recording Studio attracted hundreds of well-known musicians including the Rolling Stones, Bonnie Raitt, The Band, R.E.M., and Marvin Lee Aday, better known as Meat Loaf.

Meat Loaf endured a paranormal encounter during the recording of his classic album "Bat out of Hell" at the Bearsville studio. The singer/songwriter claims that in 1976, while he and producer Todd Rundgren worked on the record, he saw a ghostly-looking woman in white in the house they occupied adjacent to the studio. Initially, the seventies rocker thought the woman a Todd Rundgren groupie, but he later learned otherwise.

On the television show *The Haunting Of,* Meat Loaf returned to the Bearsville recording studios to confront the ghostly encounter that haunted him for decades. During the filming of the show, multiple equipment failures occurred and the crew attributed the glitches to supernatural forces.

Soon after his initial sighting, a second encounter involved a more malicious entity that slammed closet doors and ripped the covers off his bed. The singer admitted he took sleeping pills out of fear.

The Haunting Of... features psychic medium Kim Russo who runs interference between the spirit world and the celebrities. Russo intuited the female ghost, the girl in white, died after falling from a tree nearby. Indeed, on September 8, 1969, one of the world's top fashion models fell to her death from a pine tree while on an outing with a group of friends. Sadly, Austrian Edna Gschopf was only 22-years-old when pronounced dead at a Kingston hospital.

Russo determined the malicious entity Meat Loaf encountered sought to discourage the artist from achieving his goals. Based on the entertainer's subsequent successes on stage and in film, it's apparent the ghost failed to diminish Meat Loaf's spirit.

Callicoon National Bank

133 Main Street
Callicoon

Callicoon's history dates to the early 1600s when the Dutch settled the area as they journeyed from the Hudson Valley. Most famously, the Erie Railroad opened in 1848 and the first steam engine came through the town. With the emergence of the railroad and its location on the Delaware River, Callicoon soon grew into a bustling community.

The 1913 Callicoon National Bank building once housed the Delaware Free Library, a branch of the Western Sullivan Public Library. The bank occupied the two-story structure, until 1967; in 1970 the library moved in.

Established in 1951, the Delaware Free library housed 600 books. Twenty years later, the library ran out of room for its 7000 volumes. The library purchased and renovated the former Callicoon National Bank building as its new home.

A member of the Sullivan Paranormal Society (SPS) often patronizes the library and felt unnerving sensations in the children's section. Consequently, the SPS arranged to conduct an investigation. The team positioned video cameras throughout the library and upon reviewing the data, a video indicated the camera in the children's section moved as if a curious *someone* picked it up and put it down.

The investigation caught the attention of the custodial staff. They informed the team they often observed a female apparition wearing a polka-dot dress roaming throughout the library. (Apparitional manifestations are the *rarest* of all supernatural phenomena).

As part of their research, the SPS investigators explored the Western Sullivan Public Library's archives and unearthed an undated newspaper photo clipping depicting the United Bank of Callicoon personnel. The photo identifies the bank's staff and includes a woman named Freda Hartz who is wearing a *polka-dot dress*.

Because Freda Hartz Molusky worked at the bank for decades, some of her relatives anonymously attended the SPS "reveal" presentation in the bank building detailing the paranormal team's investigation of the library. During the program, Freda's clan was caught by surprise to hear Barbara O'Rourke present the team's findings, which included the female spirit in the polka dot dress identified as their relative!

Western Hotel

22 Upper Main Street
Callicoon

"The shock of an unnatural death sends invisible
being in a mad turmoil and makes adjustment to
a new environment impossible for a while."
—Jane Sherwood, *A Country Beyond*

In 1921, Laura Darling Kahl was shot to death on the front steps of the Western Hotel by her husband Peter. Ever since that fateful day, haunted happenings at the hotel support the idea Laura's spirit lingers at the spot where she passed away.

Around 1913, Laura's father, Howard Darling, hired a young man named Peter Kahl as the hotel's barkeep. Two years later, he and Laura married. Kahl eventually became the hotel's manager, and upon Howard Darling's death in 1920, Peter and Laura became the proprietors.

Laura was attractive, flirtatious, and an accomplished musician. Her playful way with male patrons irritated her jealous husband and the couple often quarreled.

When 25-year-old engineer George Turner arrived in town to install a refrigeration system in the local market, he caught Laura's eye. The tension between Laura and her husband escalated over her obvious attraction to the newcomer. Turner often dined at the Western and frequented the hotel bar. Peter Kahl disliked the attention Laura and Turner lavished on each other, to put it mildly.

On Saturday, April 3, 1921, Laura attended a nearby dance with some friends, including Turner, against her husband's wishes. Kahl even showed up at the dance to take her home but Laura refused to leave.

The seething Kahl returned to the hotel and, with a gun in hand, fumed as he awaited Laura's arrival. Upon her return at three a.m., a heated argument ensued and Kahl pulled the trigger on his wife shooting her in the head. He aimed the pistol at Turner but horrified onlookers wrestled Kahl to the ground thwarting more carnage. The twenty-nine-year-old woman perished inside the hotel moments later.

Peter Kahl was arrested and charged with first-degree murder in Sullivan County. The trial lasted five days, the jury deliberated less than three hours, and Peter Kahl was found not guilty.

Shortly after the trial, eerie happenings started to occur in the hotel. Guests heard the sound of footsteps and an indistinct female voice. Doors mysteriously opened and closed on their own. Quite oddly, only male guests experienced the anomalies; female guests seemed oblivious to the unusual activity.

In the *Times Herald-Record*, historian John Conway related the experiences of one particular guest... After the gentleman retired to his room for the night, the air temperature dropped significantly. When the guest awoke in the morning he found the window he left open was closed and an extra blanket on his bed. Thinking the maid used her pass key to open the door and tend to his needs, he thanked her but she denied performing the niceties.

Stories of Laura's ghost proliferated for over six decades. They ceased in the 1980s when the hotel owners decided knowledge of its resident spirit would deter customers.

These days a haunted reputation draws curiosity and spirit seekers boosting any establishment's revenues.

Many feel Laura Darling Kahl's spirit remains earth-bound and will continue to linger until the guilty party is held accountable and justice is served.

Waitress Shot to Death

Callicoon's Western Hotel witnessed not one, but two murders. On April 13th, 2008, eighty-seven years to the month of Laura Darling Kahl's murder, a bar patron and championship shooter chatted with Joe Naughton, the Western's owner. Actress Lori Schubeler worked behind the bar as Naughton showed off his personal firearms collection. While handling a semi-automatic handgun, Naughton accidentally discharged the weapon. The bullet hit Schubeler in the chest, killing her at 12:30 a.m. She was 41 years old. Unlike Peter Kahl, Naughton was convicted of the shooting. Naughton's accidental crime netted six months in jail, a five-year probation, 500 hours of community service and a prohibition to own firearms again.

Thomas Cole House

218 Spring Street
Catskill

In 1925, Thomas Cole, the English-born founder of the Hudson River School of painting, made his first sketching trip to the Catskills. The paintings that followed created a sensation in the New York art world and influenced a host of other young, talented American artists.

In 1832, he rented an outbuilding at Cedar Grove, now the Thomas Cole National Historic Site, and established his studio. On November 22, 1836, Cole and Maria Bartow, his landlord's niece, married at Cedar Grove. The couple moved into a suite of rooms on the second floor.

On February 6, 1848, Cole attended church with his family. After lunch, he complained of fatigue. An attack of pleurisy and congestion of his lungs followed and Thomas Cole died at home five days later.

Today, Cole's house and studio serve as a museum and National Historic Site dedicated to his life and to the legacy of the Hudson River painters.

Going to the studio where the self-taught artist created some of his most hauntingly beautiful works, provides views of the inspiring landscapes. A visit may also elicit an encounter with Thomas Cole's spirit as well.

The romantic artist wrote over one hundred poems about art and nature during his lifetime. In 1834, he wrote:

"O Cedar Grove! When'er I think to part
From thine all peaceful shades my aching heart
Is like to his who leaves some blessed shore
A weeping exile ne'er to see it more."

Clearly, the artist cherished his beloved home. Perhaps this is why it's suspected he may still be in residence.

In *Hudson Valley Haunts*, Linda Zimmerman cites the experience of a docent who is also an artist herself. While painting on the porch at Cedar Grove, she clearly sighted Thomas Cole and his wife looking out a window of the

Museum Room as if admiring the views. The room was locked and vacant at the time.

Some staffers and tourists hear footsteps and faint, indistinct voices having a conversation. A visiting psychic discerned Cole painting in his studio and Maria in the house with the children.

Some claim hauntings to be displacements in time during which the past can be experienced. In his study, *How to Hunt Ghosts: A Practical Guide,* author Joshua P. Warren says, "Regardless of exactly how time functions, paranormal imprints show us that, for whatever reason, events can be recorded in an environment."

Whatever the cause of the mystical phenomena at Cedar Grove, it's an offshoot of Thomas Cole's strong attachment to the people and place he loved. His passion is evident in his paintings as well and they embody the artist's true spirit.

Bull's Head Inn

105 Park Place
Cobleskill

The oldest building in the Village of Cobleskill is also its most haunted. George Ferster arrived in the Schoharie Valley in 1752 and built a log home near the Cobleskill Creek. His log cabin burned to the ground *twice* during the French and Indian War. Undaunted, Ferster rebuilt both times. The last reconstruction developed into a tavern and he sold the property to a German immigrant, Lambert Lawyer.

During Lawyer's tenancy, the building burned again. In 1802, Seth Wakeman acquired the new structure and named his place the Bull's Head Inn. The inn served as a town hall, a courthouse, and for a time, a Masonic Lodge before 1839.

John Stacy, a notoriously heavy drinker, took ownership of 105 Park Place in 1920. His wife Grace, was a member of good standing in the Women's Christian Temperance Union and an avid prohibitionist.

In 1964, owner Monty Allen established a bar in Grace's former bedroom. Evidently, the remodel roused a raging Grace from her grave and the haunting commenced.

Countless times, the wait staff observed napkins and silverware tossed off tables, glasses knocked over and salt and pepper shakers go missing. Seems like the long-dead teetotaler is throwing temper (ance) tantrums! A female apparition in a long white dress wanders through the dining room late at night. She drifts *through* the tables, chairs, and walls.

To this day patrons report the appearance of strange orbs of light. Shadows appear and vague forms materialize in mirrors. Staffers hear footsteps and other noises upstairs when the floor is vacant. Seeing strangers guzzle in her former home gets Grace's ghost going. Captain's chairs swivel without explanation and a decorative, disconnected crank-style phone sometimes rings.

The spirit's eerie behavior intensifies when late-night revelers are reluctant to leave the old-time watering hole. Seems Grace's ghost is a self-appointed spirit bouncer.

Frisbee House

46549 State Highway 10
Delhi

Historic buildings hold their secrets close. Can the creaks and groans within their walls be less due to age and more because of lingering spirits?

In 1797, Gideon Frisbee (1758–1828) built a house that eventually grew into a community gathering place, an inn/tavern, and courthouse that hosted the first meeting of the Delaware County Supervisors Committee. Over its long existence, the building has witnessed many other significant historical events. The homestead bore witness to sorrow as well so it's no wonder unexplainable and unsettling events transpire in the celebrated home.

In 1804, Hulda Gideon passed away in the house leaving her husband and six children behind. Five years later, Gideon and his second wife lost their infant son George.

Staffers and visitors believe some former inhabitants stay behind haunting the historic home. Inexplicable noises resound and the uncomfortable sensation of being watched are among the telltale signs of their presence. The addition, built on the back of the home, houses the nursery. This room is the most unnerving and is avoided at all costs. A young boy visiting the property observed a ghost sitting in the nursery's rocking chair—the chair where his mother once rocked baby George.

Ghosts can become stuck when they feel responsible for someone on earth, particularly a baby or child. Often a departed mother will be unable to leave her children, the maternal instinct can supersede death, and the mother's spirit will stay to watch over her family until she is convinced of their safety. Mothers can still influence, comfort and protect as a spirit on the other side.

The property surrounding the centerpiece of the Delaware County Historical Association includes the original barns, Frisbee family cemetery, and outbuildings, as well as numerous 19th-century buildings relocated to the site. These include a blacksmith shop, one-room schoolhouse, a gun shop, and a turnpike tollgate house. In addition, exhibit galleries, research library and archives, gift/book shop and nature trail exist.

The historical association also offers a series of Twilight Lantern Tours where guests can learn more about the historic site's eerie elements.

Point Lookout
Mountain Inn

7604 NY Route 23
East Windham

Today's Captain's Inn Point Lookout, previously known as the Point Lookout Mountain Inn, was allegedly the site of a murder. More famously, the tavern perched on Point Lookout became a popular Catskill Mountain destination attracting patrons for decades because of the site's spectacular five-state view. On a clear day, the panorama encompasses New York State's Helderberg Mountains, Massachusetts' Berkshire Mountains, Vermont's Green Mountains, the White Mountains of New Hampshire and the Connecticut Valley.

Located 1900 feet above sea level, the location welcomed travelers for centuries. The Mohican tribe sojourned at the spot en route to their favored hunting grounds in the highlands. Eventually, a stagecoach stop was built on the site. In the 1920s, an entrepreneur built a seasonal snack bar, gift shop and outdoor decks mounted with viewing telescopes. Most impressive was the tower erected to provide a more spectacular view. Even President Franklin Delano Roosevelt visited Point Lookout.

In 1965, a fire destroyed the original inn. The new structure featured more lodging and a larger restaurant.

Point Lookout Inn's history includes a dark chapter, however. One night, a homicide occurred in Room 12 according to Lisa La Monica, the author of *Haunted Catskills*. A couple checked into the now infamous room. A quarrel ensued resulting in the male guest murdering his female companion. The woman's body went undiscovered for days. No police record of this alleged slaying exists.

Room 12's tainted past set in motion strange happenings in the space such as a putrid stench, voices and flickering lights as reported by guests. Lodgers even felt the effects of the supposed tragedy that occurred. Oddly, their demeanor seemed to change—for the worse. One mild-mannered guest became extremely agitated over the smell in the room to the point where the manager called the authorities who physically removed the out-of-control occupant. Subsequent to his visit, the one-time guest apologized and explained something uncontrollable overwhelmed him.

As years went on, several staffers noticed unusual happenings as well, including the ever-pervading foul odor. The television and lights went on and housekeepers heard the voices too.

When new owners, Lauren and Ron, purchased the inn, their cat behaved strangely and they became quite aware of the odor in Room 12. They thoroughly cleaned the room over and over again. They brought in expert contractors to determine the cause of the smell but to no avail. No one could unearth the source of the stench.

In 2011, a crew from the Animal Planet TV channel visited the hotel to film an episode for *The Haunted* series. The Pennsylvania Paranormal Association investigated the premises and hired two cadaver dogs who went straight to the corner of Room 12, a positive indication of a death in the room.

Psychic medium Virginia Centrillo contacted the spirit of the murder victim and successfully persuaded the female spirit to cross over to the unseen world. Thankfully, this paranormal intervention appeased the spirit and solved the problem… the stench disappeared and harmony now pervaded the premises.

Fantinekill Cemetery

The Catskill Mountain region, with so many historical locations, is a ghost hunting treasure trove. At
present, a large number of people and organizations enjoy
visiting and researching reputedly haunted sites. Thousands
devote their weekends to exploring and investigating spirited locations.

Paranormal investigators utilize a vast array of high-
tech equipment to unearth spirits. For instance, photographs taken with digital cameras can offer convincing

evidence; digital sound recordings of electronic voice phenomenon (EVP) provide additional proof. In many cases, professional evidential mediums belong to ghost hunting groups and/or the members themselves sometimes possess mediumship abilities. Their communications with the spirit world advance the research as well as the philosophy of life after life.

The Sullivan Paranormal Society (SPS) is a volunteer group based in Sullivan County. Their mission is to investigate the paranormal in an attempt to prove its existence. When the SPS visited the Fantinekill Cemetery, the group "drove in with the hope of exploring some local history and left with more than we knew."

The society's co-founder, Barbara O'Rourke, said: "Sensitivities heightened as a few in our group 'noticed' we weren't alone, and here and there we could not shake the 'creepy' feeling that we all knew too well. Many photos were taken, along with audio and video recordings. One team member captured an astounding EVP. Using an Instagram video, the investigator unintentionally picked up a disembodied voice saying, "*Sightseeing, are we?*"

A second visit to the graveyard did not disappoint. Intuitive sensations flooded Barbara as she conducted an EVP session beside an older, toppled tombstone. She asked the spirits, *"Are you here?"* The investigator received an answer as she later listened to the audio playback during evidence review, *"Behind you"* came the eerie response!

Shadowland Theatre

157 Canal Street
Ellenville

Across the globe, theaters are notoriously haunted. And with the amount of drama, superstition, and ego associated with stagecraft, it's no wonder. Many playhouses enact rituals to appease the resident ghost(s). For example, London's Palace Theatre, leaves seats empty to accommodate the spirits. Theaters traditionally close one day per week to avoid any ghostly retribution.

Another superstition is every theater installs a "ghost light." The ghost light keeps the theatre ghost company overnight. The practice originated because when all the lights go out, the ghost feels abandoned and instigates accidents on the set. The ghost light allows the spirits to perform on stage if they so desire. Appeasing the spirits prevents a jinx on the theater or its productions.

Billed as the Catskills' "cultural gem," the Shadowland Theatre opened on July 3, 1920, as an art-deco movie and vaudeville house. Originally seating 900, substantial renovations completely rebuilt the old theater's interior. Preserving most of the art-deco features, a tiered, 186 seat, semi-thrust stage was installed providing all seats within 35 feet of the stage clear sightlines.

Elusive, shadowy forms flit through the playhouse along with disembodied footsteps. Objects frequently go missing. While building a set, a construction worker left his hammer on the stage at quitting time. The next day he looked all over for the tool and eventually located the hammer hanging from the ceiling lighting framework 40 feet overhead.

Decades ago a woman committed suicide in the Shadowland. She attended a performance and must have hid inside overnight because the next morning workers found her lifeless body hanging above the balcony. Afterward, those with heightened senses sighted the woman's spirit still swinging. A woman's voice and her whispers echoed in the balcony as well.

Doors open and close on their own in the restroom and the taps turn on by themselves. The sound of heavy footsteps walking across the stage creates an eerie tingling sensation.

Psychic and psychometrist, Barbara Bleitzhofer observed a spectral man take a seat in the third row from the rear. When she went to psychically examine the area, she felt pushed by unseen hands.

Theater ghosts… what better way to spend the afterlife, being entertained on a regular basis and interacting with hundreds of different people in a variety of ways…

Shawangunk Country Club

38 Country Club Road
Ellenville

Eburn Haight originally owned the Shawangunk Country Club property. Haight initially erected a modest family home but his son, David, desired a larger dwelling in which to celebrate his daughter Caroline's wedding.

David considered Caroline so beautiful that he placed her in front of a mirror so she could be viewed from all angles during her 1851 marriage ceremony.

According to legend, one day as David and his younger brother Jesse walked the farm, Jesse observed an exquisite pine tree and told David to bury him by the tree when he died. A short time later, Jesse contracted diphtheria and passed away. According to his wishes, his body was interred near the conifer.

In 1838, Eburn Haight deeded one acre of the farm to the Methodist Church "to be used as a Public Burial Yard for the Village of Ellenville and its vicinity." Jesse's grave, near the pine tree, became the first burial in what developed into the Old Ellenville Cemetery. Also known as the Leurenkill Cemetery, gravestones indicate burials as early as 1807 and includes the burial places of many Civil War soldiers.

The Shawangunk Country Club purchased the original Haight Farm in 1927. The present clubhouse encompasses David Haight's home. Witnesses claimed to see a young boy's pale apparition roaming in the vicinity of the golf club.

Ruby's Hotel

3689 County Route 67
Freehold

Ruby's Hotel features a restaurant, two-room boutique hotel and a fine art gallery located above the restaurant. Once the Meyer Hotel, Ruby's rooms display a vintage décor. The 1800 architectural gem is furnished with original tables, chairs, lighting fixtures, bar and art deco soda fountain.

When the building sat vacant, passersby sighted a dark-haired woman looking out an attic window. The proprietors call the spirit "Ruby." Since that time, some visitors also see the woman strolling through the place, according to co-owner Chef Ana Sporer who worked at The Pierre in Manhattan and taught at the New York Restaurant School and the Institute of Culinary Education.

The sound of mysterious footsteps late at night on the stairs and upper floorboards in the hallway resonate in the building. Without reason, Ana discerns a coconut scent pervading the upstairs and once she and her husband, Frank, heard a phantom "meow."

In *The Ghosts of New York, Volume Two*, David J. Pitkin writes the Sporers' friend, Frank Broderick, died at twenty-eight years of age. To honor their friend and one-time bartender, the Sporers placed a photo behind the bar. As a bit of fun, Ana wedged a candy bar behind the picture for him. A few days later when Ana checked, the candy bar was gone! How could this be? No one knew about the sweet treat.

The second-floor art gallery is named after Broderick and the Sporers feel his presence still lingers. Ana and friends who overnighted in the place experienced lucid dreams where Broderick appeared to them conveying the message he lives on.

During the Broderick Art Gallery opening night, one of Pitkin's friends in attendance discerned Broderick's proud spirit. He also intuited other male and female presences. The spirits of the artists whose work was on display perhaps? Pitkin himself perceived the spirit of a circa 1900s era housekeeper/farmer's wife who telepathically communicated she cleaned the building to earn extra cash.

Pitkin and friends observed many spirts in the age-old structure. Hundreds of individuals passed through its doors when the building operated as Meyer's Hotel so it's hard to identify the individual spirits or speculate as to their reasons for staying behind.

Inconspicuous to patrons, Ruby's spirits remind us to remember those who went before and the ones who chose to stay.

Burn Brae Mansion

In 1907, Margaret Ross MacKenzie Elkin built Burn Brae Mansion as part of George Ross MacKenzie's estate. MacKenzie became the third president of the Singer Sewing Machine Company and confidant to Isaac Singer, the company's founder.

Upon George's death in 1892, seven of his children built elaborate summer mansions in Glen Spey. Margaret and Charles Elkin's Burn Brae Mansion remains one of three still surviving. Margaret was a philanthropist and Charles, engineer, inventor, and accomplished organist, also operated a spring water bottling works on the wooded property.

Over the years, Burn Brae Mansion served as a boarding house, a tea room during prohibition and an inn. Owners, Mike and Pat Fraysse, restored the home to its original character. They currently operate the house as a bed and breakfast inn, along with a 12-room motel sited on the former horse stables.

For over four decades, guests and owners of this Victorian manse reported ghost sightings, unexplained occurrences and general feelings of an otherworldly presence. Sounds of doors opening and slamming, disembodied children's voices and balls bouncing on their own, to cite a few. Visitors also often report the distinct sound of organ music yet no organ exists in the dwelling.

Most astonishing, three apparitions walked the building—a woman in white, a man wearing 19th century clothing and another male specter dressed in overalls. More recently, an elderly couple in their 90s, the Hapijs, both died in the house. Guests say they can still see them from the front yard playing chess by the big window, hear his classical music and smell her daily baking.

Burn Brae Mansion underwent restoration in preparation for its 100th anniversary celebration. Following the renovations, the original servants' quarters, now named the Singer Suite and Elkin Room, and the adjoining guest rooms, now named the MacKenzie Suite, opened to the public. Shortly after reopening, overnight guests reported mysterious sights and sounds during their visit.

During an investigation, South Jersey Ghost Researchers found evidence "off the charts compared to an average investigation," according to Burn Brae's website. On a beautiful summer night, fourteen SJGR team members investigated the mansion using motion sensors, digital cameras, digital voice recorders and infrared thermometers.

Nearly 200 photos revealed anomalies as did two video recordings and five motion sensor readings. The team captured 47 occurrences of electronic voice phenomena (EVP) and 32 anomalous electromagnetic field (EMF) readings. The team sensed inexplicable cold spots and emotional swings.

The haunted Burn Brae Mansion can be reserved for paranormal investigations upon request and availability.

Haines Falls Railroad Station

5132 Route 23A
Haines Falls

During the early 19th century, waterways formed New York's principal transportation network. By the end of the Civil War, however, railroads pre-empted water travel as the preferred method of conveyance for coal and commercial goods throughout the area and guided vacationers to the Catskills' grand lodges.

By the mid-19th century, the Hudson River School painters and their landscape depictions of mountain grandeur, made the eastern Catskills a top vacation destination for travelers from around the world. The northern Catskills were served by the Catskill Mountain Branch of the Ulster and Delaware Railroad (U&D).

At its peak, the U&D railroad, known as the "Only All-Rail Route to the Catskill Mountains," connected 107 miles of mountain terrain on its trek from Kingston, through the Catskill Mountains, to Oneonta.

Eventually, the U&D required a larger station to accommodate the swell of well-to-do travelers headed for the Catskill Mountain House, Laurel House, and the Hotel Kaaterskill, among others.

In 1932, economic extremes forced the U&D Railroad to sell to the New York Central Railroad and the Haines Falls station became a summer-only stop.

The Great Depression left some without funds to purchase train tickets while wealthier members of society travelled by car. The automobile caused Catskill Mountain tourism to dwindle as travelers sought different venues. The U&D railroad discontinued passenger service. With more than 60 million cars on the road by 1958, the automobile had replaced the train as the preferred transportation mode. The railroad declared bankruptcy and abandoned the station.

A private investor acquired the property and converted the station into rental apartments. One tenant felt pulled to live in the repurposed building and she rented the space previously occupied by a schoolteacher. One year into her tenancy, she heard piano music yet she could not determine the music's source. Family and friends visiting the apartment also heard the phantom melodies.

Over time, she came to hear other inexplicable noises like someone laughing, for instance, and she determined the dwelling held a benign and happy spirit, one that felt like a comforting presence.

According to author David Pitkin in *New York State Ghosts, Volume Two*, one night the tenant heard a crash that woke her up. A curtain rod somehow managed to lift out of its u-shaped brackets and fall to the floor. The woman noticed a mist rising from the carpet, although she soon horribly realized the vapor was smoke! Her space heater caused the rug to catch fire. The result could have been tragic without the curtain rod falling to wake her up. Is this an act of spirit intercession?

In 1996, the Mountain Top Historical Society acquired the station and restored the structure which now serves as its headquarters.

Kaaterskill Falls

"Is that a being of life, that moves
Where the crystal battlements rise?
A maiden watching the moon she loves,
At the twilight hour, with pensive eyes?
Was that a garment which seemed to gleam
Betwixt the eye and the falling stream?"

—William Cullen Bryant, "Catterskill Falls"

On weekends, thousands of people hike the well-worn trail to the base of Kaaterskill Falls, a two-stage waterfall on Spruce Creek. The double cascade totals 260 feet in height is the tallest waterfall in New York State. The popular landmark, one of America's oldest tourist attractions, was portrayed as a primeval paradise and romanticized in many 19th century books, essays, poems and paintings.

In 1819, Washington Irving depicted the cascading water in "Rip Van Winkle." Beginning with Thomas Cole in 1825, the falls inspired the Hudson River School of landscape painters. The falls also inspired the poem "Catterskill Falls" by William Cullen Bryant.

At the height of their popularity, a dam was erected at the crest to regulate the flow of the water in scheduled "performances" at which spectators were charged an admission fee to witness the falls in action.

Today the falls flow of their own accord. Remnants of their heyday remain in the foundations of long-gone hotels and a mysterious engraving dated June, 1868.

On the left side of the falls, halfway between the middle and top level exists a worn engraving dedicated to the "Bayard of Dogs," a tragic story of a dog's devotion to his master, even unto death. The plague commemorates "Vite," who leaped to his death from the top of the falls attempting to reach his master down below.

Legend says, on June 19th of every year, as the clock strikes the witching hour, the spaniel's spirit haunts the vicinity of the falls. A succession of short, sharp barks is heard followed by the flight of the canine's apparition over the falls into the precipice and after that a prolonged howl.

***Note well!** The number of deaths at Kaaterskill Falls is staggering. Nearly every year at least one person who ignores the signs warning to climb up to the upper basin, falls and dies. If you fall off the top of Kaaterskill Falls, the probability of surviving is virtually zero. Over the span of 200 years, only one person survived a fall. Always keep safety your number one priority.*

Depuy Canal House

1315 Main Street
High Falls

In 1797, prominent citizen Simeon DePuy, built a stone structure to serve as his Stone House Tavern. In 1827, Delaware & Hudson (D & H) commenced operations ushering in a new era of cargo and coal transport. DePuy's tavern occupied the site of Lock 16. His business flourished as the canal men refueled at the eatery.

The D & H Canal Company acquired the building in 1850 and maintained offices at the site until 1898.

The coming of the railroad sounded the death knell for canal transport. Rail travel provided cheaper and faster transport and operated in all seasons. At the turn of the 20th century, the canal closed permanently and the canal house sat empty.

In 1964, John Novi, a D & H Canal enthusiast, purchased the former Stone House Tavern housed in the old, stone building. Over the next few years the High Falls resident restored the structure and for over 40 years operated a four-star restaurant known as the Depuy Canal House.

During Novi's tenancy, paranormal commotion became the norm. In *Hudson Valley Haunts*, author Linda Zimmerman told the tales of incredible haunting activity. Novi resided upstairs and he regularly heard footsteps below as if someone went about closing up for the night. Often he'd find locked doors wide open and faucets spouting water. Lights glowed below closed doors accompanied by inexplicable sounds. One night the light became so bright he swore he'd find a fire blazing in the fireplace. When he entered the room, no light shone whatsoever.

Does Simeon DePuy's spirit remain in residence to watch over the place? If so, he is in store for big changes that will preserve the structure's integrity and longevity.

In 2015, the Delaware & Hudson Canal Historical Society acquired the historic property and extensive work is underway to prepare the building as a museum of the D & H Canal's heyday. The new museum will include a visitor center to serve as a gateway to the area's extensive trail systems and numerous tourist attractions.

We humans tend to resist change. The same is true for ghosts, once mortal like us, of course. Maybe new paranormal stories will emerge as a result of the extensive restoration. Ghosts notoriously act up when their environment is tampered with... stay tuned.

"But what does 'dead' really mean, anyway? For me, it seems to refer simply to 'being permanently away from the body,' as there are so many recorded instances of personalities continuing on, at least for a while after the body's death."
—David J. Pitkin

Highland Public Library

30 Church Street
Highland

Each community establishes its library for different reasons. Many small-town libraries founded in the early 20th century originated as community reading rooms in answer to local women's need for a place to congregate. Such is the case with the Highland Public Library, which celebrated its 100th anniversary in 2015.

During the age of the woman's suffrage movement, reading rooms and libraries became welcome refuges for women, an oasis where they could freely exercise their intellect.

By 1920, the library required a larger, permanent space to meet the growing demand so the trustees purchased the former dental office of Dr. Caspar Ganse on the corner of Main and Church streets. The library continued to grow and in 1929 relocated directly across the street at 30 Church Street, the former home of Dr. Ganse and his wife, Georgianna.

Librarian Sara Ottaviano shared that doors slam without cause, disturbing the hushed atmosphere. Window blinds open on their own. Books mysteriously fall from shelves. Once a quarter appeared out of nowhere and rolled along the floor.

Most attribute the perplexing activity to Georgianna's spirit. One passerby even sighted a female apparition in the attic window after hours.

Some suggest the revenant could be artist Lillian Spencer, however. According to town historian Terry Scott, the local artist bartered some of her paintings for dental services during financial hardship. One of her canvasses still hangs in the library.

Hurley Historic District

In 1662, Peter Stuyvesant established the village of Niew Dorp on the site of an earlier Native American settlement. The following year, the Esopus Wars ensued. The Esopus raided the village and burned the settlers' wooden homes to the ground. In 1669, the village, since acquired by the English, resettled the abandoned village and renamed the colony Hurley after the new governor's ancestral home. This time the colonists rebuilt using stone.

On October 16, 1777, the British burned Kingston which served as New York's capitol. Many fled to Hurley and the Van Deusen House became the capitol temporarily.

Hurley's Main Street is listed on the National Register of Historic Sites; some of the stone houses served as residences for more than 300 years. Main Street is a step back in time possessing "the oldest concentration of privately owned stone houses in the United States."

The Van Deusen House possesses a long haunted history. In fact, one prior resident installed a heavy duty latch to keep the ghosts out! While working on refurbishing the house, one owner felt the distinct sensation of someone watching him. Some other visitors in the home also sensed the ethereal presence. Another inhabitant awoke to find a Native American standing over her bed. Other haunting activity in the Van Deusen House includes the usual phantom fare of disembodied noises, footsteps on the stairs and doors opening and closing—all experienced by family members and friends alike.

On October 10, 1777, Lieutenant Daniel Taylor was captured in southern Ulster County, carrying a missive from General Henry Clinton to General John Burgoyne. He traveled in civilian clothes on horseback carrying messages between various units of the British Army. Ordinarily, such messengers from either side did not constitute spying. However, the British captured Nathan Hale of Connecticut a year earlier and hanged him as a spy. Lt. Taylor was tried by mostly Connecticut officers and condemned to be hanged.

American troops left Connecticut to defend Kingston from the British and took Taylor with them. Taylor was held in Hurley's Dumond House until the next morning when he was hanged from a sweet apple tree on School-house Lane.

His body hung roadside for two days to warn passing troops and British sympathizers. Taylor's remains were buried at the site and, according to legend, relocated beneath a tavern's door so patrons would walk over his body. (His family ultimately exhumed the body and reinterred the lieutenant in a private site).

Many locals claim a shadowy black form still lurks about the town and it's believed Lieutenant Taylor is the wraith wandering the streets. One resident thought he struck the dark figure while driving but when he exited his car, he saw no one. In later life, he discovered others experienced similar incidents.

Another Hurley Street house is haunted by a little girl who calls out "Momma!" and the rocking chair frequently rocks on its own. One more house possesses a male spirit who once spoke to a little girl living in the home. The inhabitants sighted his specter walk across a room and through the wall.

In 1776, Cornelius D. Wynkoop, an "Associator" of Hurley, received a promotion to Colonel. In 1792, the retired colonel perished in his residence from a brutal ax attack. One of his slaves named Charles, mistakenly murdered his master when Wynkoop sought to calm the servant after he became enraged at his mistreatment by other household members. Charles hanged for the crime on July

3, 1793. The remains of an adolescent girl were unearthed on the Wynkoop House property and it's suspected she also suffered a violent death at the site.

In this era of deeply seeded superstition, Dutch settlers viewed witches and black magic as a threat hanging over the land like a dark cloud. The lower level of the 1735 Polly Crispell Cottage once served as a blacksmith shop. The chimneys held iron spikes the Dutch believed would keep out witches and evil spirits.

Old Hurley Burial Grounds is one of the oldest in Ulster County and contains many field stones, some engraved in Dutch; many bear no inscriptions. The cemetery is populated with the remains of its earliest settlers. "Spook Hole" exists behind the graveyard. According to legend, the area is so named because witches and ghosts tended to gather in the gully near the Elmendorf house. One Hurley gentleman spotted a ghost leaning against a fence one night; his horse refused to walk past the spot.

Gitty Ten Eyck Pauling is buried in the cemetery. Her gravestone is marked with a skull and crossbones—the marking of a witch. Some hear rustling in the bushes near her grave and observe a blue light.

Each year on the second Saturday in July, some of the private homes open to the public. The time spent in each house is at your discretion. For more spookiness, Hurley Heritage Society "Brings out the Dead" with its Annual Ghost Walk every October.

Sullivan County Museum

The Hurleyville School House is home to the Sullivan County Historical Society & Museum. Built in 1912, the schoolhouse served as a grammar school and later expanded to include the high school grades. The structure continued to be used as a school until 1967.

The Hurleyville Fire Department became the next owner of the building and in 1971, Sullivan County acquired the edifice. In addition to housing the historical society museum and archives, the building also serves as the headquarters for the Sullivan County Dramatic Workshop and the Frederick A. Cook Society.

On multiple occasions, the Sullivan Paranormal Society (SPS) investigated the museum due to feelings of unease experienced in the building.

The historical society utilizes an upper floor for storage. One room holds old uniforms, wedding dresses and other odd bits of apparel. The room also contains mannequins. (Just the word "mannequin" makes this writer start to sweat!). As the team set up cameras in the space and conducted an electronic voice phenomena (EVP) session, some members commented out loud about the creepy feeling in the mannequin-filled room. Upon review of the data collected during the investigation, the team clearly heard a disembodied voice loudly whisper, *"I love this room."*

On each occasion, the SPS recorded a lot of EVPs. Because of the building's association with polar explorer Frederick A. Cook, a team member addressed any "explorers in spirit" who might be attracted to the location. When asked, *"What kind of animals did you see?"* a spirit voice distinctly answered, *"A duck."*

Stone Arch Bridge

25 Stone Arch Road
Kenoza Lake

*"The spirit of a man lives on who has
died by violence before his time."*

—Dion Fortune

On January 19, 1892, George Markert was murdered upon the stone arch bridge by Adam Heidt and his son Joseph. Markert was a successful businessman while his brother-in-law Adam was an uneducated and ineffective farmer and a superstitious man. Heidt viewed his brother-in-law's success and his own failures as the work of the devil.

When Heidt's cows stopped producing milk and his crops failed to yield and his health took a turn for the worse, he became convinced Markert practiced witchcraft. He determined Markert placed a curse on him when he patted his back three times. When Heidt confronted Markert about the hex, he laughed in his face.

Heidt's life continued to spiral downward and he felt something must be done. In order to negate the curse, Heidt determined his nemesis needed to be killed by three separate methods.

On a cold January night, Heidt followed Markert to the local tavern. After several drinks, witnesses claimed the two men left together. It was the last time George Markert was seen alive.

As the men crossed the stone arch bridge over Callicoon Creek—folklore holds witches and warlocks hold no power when positioned over running water—a third man, Heidt's eldest son, Joseph emerged from the woods. They shot Markert in the head, clubbed him repeatedly and tossed his body into the frigid water.

When Markert's mutilated body turned up a few days later, the Heidts admitted to the deed and pled self-defense against a practitioner of the dark arts.

Adam Heidt was found guilty by reason of insanity and committed to a state hospital where he died five years later. Joseph Heidt was convicted of murder in the second degree and sentenced to life in prison.

Almost immediately, locals reported the eerie sighting of Markert's ghost on the stone arch bridge, usually on cold winter nights. The sightings continue to this day.

Also on a cold January night, the Sullivan Paranormal Society utilized a "ghost box" to communicate with George Markert. A ghost box is a communication tool used by some paranormal investigators to connect with those on the other side. Typically, the device is a modified portable radio that creates white noise enabling the entities to manipulate energy and create words and sentences. When Barbara O'Rourke asked, "Do you know who murdered you,

George?" The device's digital display read, "Adam." Upon audio playback, the team distinctly heard a male voice say *"Adam."* Once *may* be coincidental but twice... now *that's* evidence!

Old Dutch Church

272 Wall Street
Kingston

The Kingston Stockade District is the original site of the mid-17th century Dutch settlement of Wiltwyck. Later the community became known as Kingston when the village passed to English rule. The Old Dutch Church sits center stage as the crux of the historic district. Established as a congregation in 1659, this is the fourth building to serve worshipers.

Religion was central to colonial life, and although settlers came to America for a number of reasons, many voyaged to New Netherland (later named New York) for religious freedom.

One of Kingston's best-known tales involves a hobgoblin entrapped in the church's steeple. In the early days of the church, the creature originally attached itself to the mast of a ship sailing the Hudson River. A clergyman and his wife returning from New York City sailed onboard. A freak storm blew up as they passed Dunderberg Mountain. A creature appeared out of nowhere and perched on the ship's foremast. The hobgoblin tried to capsize the boat as it navigated the turbulent waters. As the clergyman prayed for safety, the hobgoblin vanished.

The next morning the hobgoblin's cap hung from the church's bell tower. In his attempt to retrieve his cap, the creature became imprisoned in the tower.

Kingston historian Edwin Ford, who's been a parishioner at Old Dutch Church since 1928, believes the story endures partly because of its intrigue. People remain fascinated with the unknown and possess an innate desire to believe there is more to this world than meets the eye. Many locals insist the tale is true because several people sense a presence in the spire and some parishioners refuse to stay in the church after dark. The church is situated atop a cemetery of more than 100 graves—with more burial places in the church's crawl space.

Although no steeple existed at the time the story emerged, Reverend Ken Walsh, a pastor at the Old Dutch Church, agrees the church is definitely haunted. When he first arrived, he experienced figures and sighted a man dressed in black and wearing a top hat, standing in his office. The pastor senses members of the original congregation still watching over the church and its parishioners.

Some say during thunderstorms, the spirit of a diminutive painter works on the steeple—his spirit visible when lightning flashes. Another steeple painter supposedly died of "painter's colic," a complication of chronic lead poisoning. In the 1980s, a steeple painter rapidly descended from the spire when he felt tapped three times on his shoulder.

Every respectable haunted house of worship possesses a ghostly organist. At the Old Dutch Church, eerie organ music originates from time to time. And lastly, to top it off, the hobgoblin supposedly added an extra line to the clock face transforming "XII" to "XIII."

Rondout Lighthouse

The Rondout Creek functioned as a deep-water port for most of the 19th and the early 20th centuries. After the opening of the Delaware & Hudson canal in 1828, the need for a lighthouse became evident to mark the entrance to Rondout Creek on the Hudson River. The canal increased trade and travel in and out of the creek; signaling the estuary became a necessity.

The Rondout Lighthouse is the last of three lighthouses marking the entrance to Rondout Creek. A wooden structure went up first. Built in 1837, storm damage required a replacement stone structure in 1867 (the old lighthouse foundation still exists). Captains complained the light failed to adequately illumine, so in 1913 construction commenced on a brick lighthouse which remains today as the Rondout/Kingston Light.

The present lighthouse became automated in the 1950s. Left abandoned, the Hudson River Maritime Museum (HRMM) initiated preservation efforts in the 1980s. In the late 1990s, the Coast Guard divested itself of the property. Still fully operational as a navigational light, the Rondout is one of seven lighthouses remaining on the Hudson River.

Accessible only by boat, Rondout Light is owned by the City of Kingston and operated by the HRMM. The City of Kingston writes: *"The 'Widow's Watch' legend is told each year after the fall equinox when it's said the lighthouse is haunted by a young bride widowed on her wedding night when her husband, the newly appointed keeper, died in a boating accident. For over a century, this young widow roams through the lighthouse at that time—still in search of her spouse."*

Old Ulster County Jail

61 Golden Hill Drive
Kingston

When it comes to haunted places, certain locales, by their very nature, seem destined for spirit unrest. Locations possessing a violent history, indelibly stained with suffering, almost inevitably pervaded by the supernatural, as if its ominous history draws these forces, absorbs and incorporates the gloom into the place.

The old Ulster County Jail at Golden Hill may be such a place if you ask Hank Vanderbeck, a retired corrections officer who insists the facility is haunted. The old jail closed in 2007 after the new state-of-the-art jail opened.

On a certain morning in 2005, Vanderbeck noticed the sudden appearance of a glowing, female figure standing to his right in the Ulster County jail. The officer is a trained observer in his corrections role and described her "perfectly white skin with long, slender fingers and real thin wrists," in an interview with journalist Paula Mitchell. The apparition stood with arms outstretched and wore a white gown glowing with an unearthly radiance. The luminous figure appeared perfectly human. As he turned his head to look at her face, however, the figure vanished.

Over the years, inmates and female officers sighted the luminous apparition in the jail's female section. The female specter emerged in the road by the infirmary according to a few nurses.

Vanderbeck worked as an Ulster County corrections officer for nearly 20 years and cites various paranormal encounters in addition to the lady in white. He's observed dark shadows passing in and out of walls and heard unnerving growls that set him on edge during his night shifts.

Ghost hunter and author Linda Zimmermann investigated the abandoned jail in 2008, calling it one of the most haunted places in the Hudson Valley. Her team positioned infrared cameras and audio recorders at paranormal hotspots… in the female cell block and second and third floors. She captured the sounds of knocking and feet dragging throughout the empty jail.

Vanderbeck experienced chilling encounters with a pair of pitch-black shapes in the third-floor recreation room. He sighted two, dark, football-shaped objects, about 3 feet long. They chased each other around the room four or five times and went out the window. An inmate claimed to see the objects tap Vanderbeck on the shoulder and the former guard felt a tingle up his back.

Female officers observed a male specter wearing coveralls in the female section; it disappeared into the walls. Other officers observed an entity dressed in a monk's habit manifest from out of nowhere and followed them around.

Another time, as a guard made his rounds, he returned to his office and found chairs placed on top of the desk. He discovered his log book inside the drawer. These pranks occurred without making a sound, according to Vanderbeck.

The trauma, pain and terror perpetrated, and experienced, by those incarcerated, often leave lasting impressions creating a ripe environment for spirits. Sometimes there is no escape—not even in death.

"Sometimes it fills my trembling heart with dread
Of the tomorrow,
To see the wraith of what I thought was dead
Its likeness borrow."
—James Berry Bensel

Senate House

296 Fair Street
Kingston

Colonel Wessel Ten Broeck built his one-story, limestone house about 1676. A century later, merchant Abraham Van Gaasbeek resided there when the first meeting of the newly elected New York State Senate convened at the house during the Revolutionary War.

One month later, the Senate fled British troops advancing from Manhattan. On October 16, 1777, British forces overtook the town plundering and setting fire to every house as retribution for Kingston's role in supporting the Revolution.

New York State acquired Abraham Van Gaasbeek's home to preserve the role Senate House played in the American Revolution. The Senate House exhibits a wide range of artwork, documents, and historical artifacts. The museum is also home to a long-held legend.

The story goes something like this… when Kingston was still known as Wiltwyck, an Englishman knocked on the Dutchman's door seeking shelter for himself and his horse. The stranger appeared well-dressed and bore a trust-worthy demeanor so the Dutchman let him in. Neither could speak the other's language, however. The young Englishman observed his surroundings and spotted a rare, old violin on the mantle. As a way to cross the linguistic divide, he picked up the instrument and played the most beautiful harmony. The old Dutchman sat enthralled and in due course, the music lulled him to sleep.

As he slept, his daughter emerged from the shadows. She secretly watched the visitor and she too became spellbound by the music. The enraptured Englishman played melody after melody for the appealing young woman until, understanding the love light in their eyes, he put aside the violin and held the young woman in his arms.

The old man awoke and found the pair in an embrace. He sent his daughter to her room and demanded the musician leave the next morning.

But the Englishman stayed in Wiltwyck and the couple met in secret. Eventually, the Dutchman found out about their clandestine trysts and ordered his daughter to be locked in her room. The despairing Englishman went sadly on his way.

Thereafter, the heartbroken daughter visited the couples' covert meeting places. She often sat by the hearth caressing the violin, the instrument they both loved. The Dutchman walked in on her and in a rage seized the instrument. The daughter went to her room and never left it again.

For two weeks she lingered between life and death. Refusing to grant her father forgiveness, she asked for one favor. She wanted the violin sealed in the side of the chimney, the place where she first met the Englishman and heard his beguiling music. The contrite father granted her wish.

Legend says the lovers' spirits still meet on the hearth before the chimney in the old Senate House and only true, loving souls can hear the Englishman's sweet music.

Franz P. Roggen House

42 Crown Street
Kingston

Colonial-era, Dutch stone houses occupy all four corners of Kingston's Crown and John Streets junction, the only intersection in the country where this is so. The Roggen House is one of the four structures situated at the historic Four Corners.

Swiss immigrant Franz P. Roggen built his Dutch Colonial style home shortly after arriving in Kingston in

1750. The property holds a unique place in the local legend that distinguishes the house from the other Dutch Colonial architecture located in the Stockade Historic District.

After the British burned Kingston in 1777 in retaliation for the town's role in supporting the American Revolution, the Roggen house stood gutted and remained in ruins until 1800. During this time the house acquired a haunted reputation when the structure's beams were used as a gallows site. The hanging beams were later incorporated into the reconstruction of the house, perhaps to ward off traitors and troublemakers.

The Underground Railroad consisted of a network of secret routes and safe houses established in the United States during the early to mid-19th century to assist African-American slaves to escape into Free states and Canada. Abolitionists and other allies, sympathetic to their cause, aided the movement. The Roggen House served as a stop on the Underground Railroad—the second-floor closet concealed fleeing slaves. This usage further attests to the building's history of serving justice.

Functioning as a residence for many years, the building is now office space and its historic exterior remains intact.

Wildmere Hotel

Lake Minnewaska

In 1879, the Cliff House overlooked Lake Minnewaska and accommodated 225 guests. After managing Mohonk Mountain House for ten years, Alfred H. Smiley purchased and developed the Cliff House separate from his Mohonk property. He oversaw the building of a second lodge called the Wildmere Hotel which accommodated 350 guests.

Cliff House was abandoned in 1972 due to maintenance costs; it burned to the ground in 1978. Wildmere closed in 1979 and fire consumed the edifice in 1986.

On occasion, he would hear the distinctive sound of a door open as he stood in a deserted hallway; he actually witnessed doors open and close as if by an invisible hand. Lewit's most vivid spooky memory, however, is a chilling one.

Sam Lewit worked at the Wildmere Hotel from 1962 until 1978. He fondly remembers the time he spent in the region and currently maintains the Lake Minnewaska website www.lakeminnewaska.org. Recently out of college, Sam initially worked as a dishwasher. Certainly not his dream job, but Sam became enchanted by Lake Minnewaska and its environs. He grew to enjoy the thousands of acres of rustic beauty and the crystal clear blue lake, rock cliffs, surrounding summerhouses, and the two beautiful 200-room Victorian lakeside hotels. He felt he lived in paradise and loved every minute.

Sam witnessed the terrible conflagration that consumed the Cliff House on the cold, snowy night of January 3, 1978. He bravely helped save some if its historic furnishing during the blaze.

During his tenure at the hotel, he experienced the supernatural first hand.

On occasion, he would hear the distinctive sound of a door open as he stood in a deserted hallway. On occasion, he actually witnessed doors open and close as if by an invisible hand. Lewit's most vivid spooky memory, however, is a chilling one.

One night, in the dead of winter, the hotel was closed as Lewit strolled the corridor where he observed the door to Room 444 mysteriously open and close. He stopped dead in his tracks and looked more closely... a light shone in the bathroom. He cautiously stepped into the room to investigate when he beheld an elderly woman brushing her long grey hair. She stood facing away from the door so he only observed the female from behind. All alone in the nether reaches of the massive, vacant hotel and observing the apparition's intimate ritual, he felt chilled to the bone and did what anyone would do...he turned and bolted for the stairs!

> *"And the ghost of that dead silence,*
> *Haunts me ever, thin and chill."*
> —William Deans Howell

Salisbury Manor

Private Residence

Usually the site of a fatal accident or murder, several places called "spook rock" exist in New York State. In this story, the location of spook rock is lost to history but the haunting tale holds strong ties to Salisbury Manor.

In 1730, William Salisbury was born in the stone mansion built by his father in 1705. Salisbury retained an indentured servant named Anna Dorothea Swarts. Anna persisted in visiting the home of a family who possessed a "bad reputation." Back in the day, the master held absolute control over their servants and was held responsible for their conduct.

On one occasion in 1755, Anna refused to return home with her master. Salisbury tied one end of the rope around the girl's waist and the other to his own—a foolhardy but not necessarily a nefarious act since he placed himself in danger as well as the girl.

The horse became frightened, Salisbury was dragged from its back and the girl met her death. Salisbury immediately informed the authorities. Indicted for murder, the case never came to trial. Salisbury received a suspended sentence until he reached the age of 99. Until that time, he wore a silken cord about his neck as a reminder of his ultimate fate. Salisbury died in 1801 at the age of 87.

A large boulder existed on the road to Salisbury Manor. Known as "spook rock," here is where the girl supposedly met her death. At midnight, on the anniversary of her demise, a ghostly gray horse with rider and girl appeared to superstitious town folks.

Please note: Salisbury Manor is privately owned. Trespassing is strictly prohibited.

Dr. Best House &
Medical Museum

1568 Clauverwie Road
Middleburgh

In 1884, Dr. Christopher S. Best (1852–1934) oversaw the building of his Italianate Victorian style house as a combination home and doctor's office. Ornamented with intricately carved woodwork and tiger maple paneling, the elegant home included a telephone, electric lighting, and an intercom system, top-notch, turn-of-the-century accoutrements.

Dr. Best's first marriage ended with the death of his wife Laura at the age of thirty-two. His second marriage was to Ursula J. Leonard who bore three children; James, (died at seven-years-of-age), Emma and Duncan. Duncan became a doctor in 1930 after graduating from the Albany Medical College; he served in the Army during World War II.

Throughout his life, community-oriented Dr. Best became involved with the Middleburgh Telephone Company, Middleburgh Central School Board of Education, Schoharie County Red Cross, the Middleburgh & Schoharie Railroad, Schoharie County coroner, St. Mark's Lutheran Church, and Rotary International. His son continued the legacy, endearing the country doctors and their families to the town.

Duncan and his father practiced medicine in the house for a total of 107 years. Upon his death in 1991, Duncan Best bequeathed his family's home to the Middleburgh Library. He asked the office be preserved and open to the public as a medical exhibit.

The volunteer Library Board of Trustees, the Rotary and Century Clubs worked tirelessly to clean and organize the contents of the home and make needed repairs. The house opened for tours in 1992.

These days, one can easily imagine the Best doctors treating patients or performing emergency surgery on the zinc-topped kitchen table. The museum's website says it best, *"...the Dr. Best collection echoes reminders of a quickly changing era. Civil War, railroad and telephone artifacts all reflect the character of this family of pioneers and visionaries. The expansive and unique collection includes thousands of bottles, automotive memorabilia, clothing and quilts, to name a few as well as the fully stocked period kitchen and state-of-the-art medical equipment."*

"The Bests never threw anything away," said Trish Bergan, the museum's director. Every item in the house was owned by one of the Best family members making the medical museum unique; everything is original and not assembled from different collections.

The family retained many cherished, interesting objects that offer visitors a glimpse into the past; walking through the doors is like stepping back in time. The Victorian household and physician's office exists as a time capsule depicting earlier days of medicine.

Viewing the museum's collection of artifacts offer insight into Victorian burial rituals and the antique medical apparatus can give one the heebie-jeebies. Considering the macabre objects stored in the house combined with the family's tragic losses, it's no wonder the paranormal pervades the property.

The house witnessed the sad deaths of Dr. Best's son, his young wife and the good doctor himself. Quite predictably, ghost hunters revealed significant activity capturing electronic voice phenomenon (EVP) and audio recordings of unearthly piano music and faraway voices.

According to Ms. Bergan, the spirits come and go, they do not remain at home all the time, however. She often hears an ethereal someone walking up and down the stairs along with the voices echoing throughout the house. One morning as the director searched the butler pantry for blueprints, someone clearly said, *"Trish."* The voice sounded as if someone stood right behind her.

Former director Bobbi Ryan, often found herself alone at the museum. Over the years, she experienced a variety of odd happenings. She once heard the giggling of a ghostly child and watched as a Victrola levitated and crashed to the floor!

A photo taken at the house showed the ghostly image of a female wearing a sunbonnet. Most identify the woman as Dr. Best's second wife Ursula. Ursula loved her garden and spent long hours outside working her flowerbeds and enjoying the fruits of her labor.

The Tri-City NY Paranormal Society, led by Gary Robusto, investigated the museum and held events in the venue many times over the years. Team members sighted shadow people on the second floor on multiple occasions and heard shuffling in the master bedroom. On most of the team's investigations, they encountered Duncan's spirit a few times each night. They detected a child-size shadow figure outside Duncan's room and walking along the hallway.

A ghost box is a paranormal research device that uses radio frequencies to communicate with spirits. When the investigators directed questions to Duncan using the ghost box, his spirit responded directly.

The ghost hunters also connected with Ursula. On one occasion, as the investigators utilized the ghost box to ask if a female spirit was present, the entity answered in the affirmative. They asked the female's name and she responded, *"Ursula."* Tri-City NY Paranormal detects the scent of roses at times—Ursula's favorite flower. She loved cultivating roses as part of her garden. Ursula's presence is often sensed in the kitchen along with the scent of violet water. Volunteers found a partially used bottle of violet water among the family's possessions.

Using a Kinect system, a skeletal mapping program that utilizes a Kinect video game sensor and laptop, Robusto picked up a strange figure on the second floor, outside the front bedroom. As lead investigator Kristi Ing walked into the exhibit room, a stick figure suddenly popped up next to her on the camera screen. Robusto directed Kristi to interact with the being by placing her hand on top of its head to determine its height. The investigator felt a cold spot where the camera indicated the stick figure stood right next to her! As Kristi moved toward the apparatus to view the stick figure on the screen, it disappeared.

There is so much to see and experience at this treasured museum. Volunteers lovingly maintain the home and organize several family-friendly events from May through December, including a paranormal event in October.

"You won't believe what's behind our doors."
—Dr. Best House & Medical Museum

Ethelbert B. Crawford Public Library

393 Broadway
Monticello

Ethelbert Baldwin Crawford (1870–1921) worked for the Erie Railroad Company as a dispatcher in Elmira. He painted as a hobby and portrayed the places he and his mother Estelle visited in the U.S. and Europe. Ethelbert studied painting with many American Impressionist painters of the time.

Ultimately, the painter's works were exhibited across the country. During his travels, Ethelbert met a woman and became engaged. Sadly, however, the couple never married because Estelle disapproved of their marriage. The censure may have contributed to the artist's suicide at aged 50.

After her son's death, Estelle approached the Metropolitan Museum of Art in New York City seeking the museum's agreement to permanently display Ethelbert's artwork. The museum declined. In 1925, Estelle passed away and bequeathed the Village of Monticello the funds to establish a library in Ethelbert's name with the understanding his paintings be exhibited at all times.

The Sullivan Paranormal Society investigated the library building at its former location at 393 Broadway. "Creepy feelings" experienced in the children's section in the basement attracted the team to the site.

EMF meters measure fluctuations in electromagnetic fields. The meter is a popular ghost hunting device because theoretically, spirits possess the ability to manipulate these fields. In the cellar, the paranormal investigators found abnormally high levels of electromagnetism.

In the past, the librarian lived on site in an apartment. An office space now occupies the former living quarter. The team recorded a lot of voices using their audio equipment and one male voice clearly says. *"What now girls?"*

Back in the day, when librarians resided here, rumor says a man broke into the residence. The librarian caught him in the act and he stabbed her outside the library. The woman survived the attack but died six months later.

Shanley Hotel

56 Main Street
Napanoch

The Shanley Hotel is one of the most famous haunted hotels in New York State. Psychic mediums travel from all over the country to explore the Shanley. In fact, this hostelry claims to be so frightening guests must sign a waiver before spending the night.

Hotel management claims a series of deaths occurred within the hotel. The tragic history includes deaths of young children. Many believe the unfortunate events provoke paranormal activity throughout the building. Guests discern children laughing and running on the stairs, doors open and close on their own and a general feeling of unease pervades the place. Paranormal investigators documented the activity with electronic voice phenomena and photos.

The hotel opened in 1845 and burned to the ground fifty years later. Rebuilt on the same site, James Louis Shanley purchased the property in 1906. Shanley and his wife Beatrice welcomed guests such as Thomas Edison and Eleanor Roosevelt, a personal friend of Mrs. Shanley.

The Shanleys suffered the loss of their three children who all died before they reached their first birthday.

In 1911, the hotel barber, who lived on-site with his family, lost his younger daughter when she fell into a well and died. A few years later, Beatrice's sister Esther died in the hotel from influenza.

It's alleged the little girl, Esther, along with Shanley's brother Andrew, haunt the hotel. Psychic medium Bill Wiand fell to his knees on the third floor when he saw a little girl sitting in a chair who said she needed help. He described the child as perhaps seven years old.

Psychic mediums Sue and Bill Wiand and Suzy Meszoly investigated the hotel's upper regions and discerned a ghost cat and the spirit of a bad-tempered, mean-spirited fellow named Tom in the attic. The team sensed a murder/suicide occurred the Blue Room.

Apparitions, drastic temperature changes, rocking chairs rocking on their own, clocks chiming, a phantom feline, disembodied footsteps, ghostly giggles, feelings of being touched, watched and/or followed and objects moving on their own describes the extent of the paranormal experienced at the Shanley.

Shanley died in 1937 and his spirit still lingers according to the hotel's website. His whistling spirit still walks the halls and climbs the stairs.

The Shanley Hotel offers lodging, ghost tours, and the chance for visitors to get up close and personal with the great beyond.

"In all my years of ghost hunting, I have never been afraid, after all, a ghost is only a fellow human being in trouble."

—Hans Holzer

Elting Memorial Library

93 Main Street
New Paltz

One of New Paltz's most visible historic buildings, the Solomon Eltinge house at the intersection of Main and North Front Streets, houses the Elting Memorial Library.

The landmark structure became a *YouTube* sensation when security cameras captured the image of an amorphous blob moving about the structure. Upon scrutiny of the camera, the image could not easily be explained by any possible technical issues.

The hubbub started on October 25th when the circulation director, noticed the library's alarm switched off. He realized the Main Street door leading into the 1802 section of the library sat ajar.

The *YouTube* video entitled "Ghost in the New Paltz Library," revealed a 33-second stretch, at approximately 3:30 am, of what the library staff described as the blurry image of an anomaly, spider, or dust mote moving across the room toward the door, eventually disappearing through the east wall. The image appeared as a meandering shadow in the oldest part of the building, where the shelves burgeon with ghost books such as, *A Gathering of Ghosts* and *Still Among the Living.*

An ofrenda, (Spanish for "offering"), is a collection of objects placed on a ritual display during the annual Mexican Día de Muertos observance. To celebrate the Day of the Dead, the library erected an ofrenda. Some contend, in a good way, that the traditional display attracted the spirit.

Carol Johnson, the coordinator of the local history and genealogy section, unearthed information about two deaths that occurred in the building. Oscar C. Hasbrouck, who owned the home, died there in 1899 of consumption. Charles V. Auchmoody, a boarder in the house, died in 1908 after suffering "a stroke of paralysis."

> *"I, like many people, believe that ghosts exist because they must tell their story to someone who can set their lives and actions into balance."*
>
> —Alex Tanous, D.D.

Historic Huguenot Street

81 Huguenot Street
New Paltz

I n 1677, twelve Huguenot families fleeing discrimination and religious persecution in France and what is
now southern Belgium founded "die Pfalz," today's New
Paltz. The settlers purchased 40,000 acres from the Esopus
Indians and constructed log huts. In 1692, stone houses
replaced the log homes. Those still standing testify to their
construction and the management of the Huguenot Historical Society.

New Paltz possesses a long, rich history since its set-
tling in 1678. Strolling along Huguenot Street is like stepping back in time. Celebrated as "America's Oldest Main
Street," the country road, amid a bustling college town, provides a look at life 300 years ago and for some, a glimpse
into another dimension. The storied neighborhood gener-
ates plenty of eerie tales spanning the centuries.

Comprised of seven stone houses, the 10-acre National
Landmark Historic District is home to an amazing number
of spirits. Listed nationwide as a Distinctive Destination by
the National Trust for Historic Preservation, the organiza-
tion offers Haunted Huguenot Street tours in October. If

you take the tour, you may experience something out of the ordinary. A couple of volunteers assert something spooky always happens on Halloween during the haunted excursion.

Abraham Hasbrouck House

Built in 1721, the Abraham Hasbrouck House is home to a male spirit and his black dog. One docent declared the spirits of Hasbrouck and his son Daniel still inhabit the house. A male presence appeared in colonial garb and was seen looking out a window of the uninhabited structure. Locals sometimes observe a spectral male walking with a dog around the property and entering the house by going *through* the door.

Over the years, the ghost stories evolved… Some cite the male spirit carries an ax into the house and is next seen in an upstairs window brandishing the weapon above his head and downward suggesting he is striking someone. Although no record of a murder in the house exists, back in the day, not every dastardly deed found its way into record books.

Hex marks or witches' marks inscribed on door latches exist here, engraved to ward off evil. The colonists were superstitious; witches or their spirits were thought to enter homes via doorways, hearths, and windows. Homeowners believed once they entered the property, the spirits would attack the inhabitants or ruin the owner's most valuable possession. Witches' marks remind us how our ancestors saw the world.

Historian Alf Evers, lived with his parents in the Abraham Hasbrouck house. His mother possessed clairvoyance—the ability to "see" things beyond the norm. In the 1920s, she insisted a child's body was buried in the basement. Alf and his father started digging to appease her and sure enough, they unearthed skeletal remains. Placed on the kitchen table, a doctor examined the bones and declared the remains those of a child. The oddest thing then happened… the bones disintegrated.

"Celestial matters do not easily lend themselves to terrestrial thinking and logic."
—Michael Tymn

DuBois Fort

O riginally constructed as a small 1½ story building, the 1705 DuBois Fort served as a fortified space for the community, although not as a defensive stronghold despite its gun ports. The edifice was enlarged to its current proportions in the late 1830s.

The DuBois family resided in the house until the 20th century, when it became an antique shop and a tea room. From 1938–1972, the structure accommodated a popular restaurant called "The Old Fort." Elsie Oates served as the proprietor and resided upstairs.

In the 1940s, Elsie sighted a tiny-wasted, female form wearing a long brown dress with an embroidered collar standing in a dimly lit hallway. Most astonishing to Elsie, the figure appeared headless. Some surmise the ghost could be the unfortunate victim of the Abraham Hasbrouck House's axman. Perhaps the entity manifested as a partial apparition.

Visible apparitions may be full-body—they look like a whole person, or they may be partial, appearing as a part of a person such as a head, an arm, or the torso. Experts assert it takes a lot of energy for a spirit to manifest into physical form, so perhaps the lady in the brown dress ran out of power, or perhaps she was viewed in process.

Subsequent to her sighting, Elsie claimed to hear strange noises in the dwelling which continued throughout her tenancy.

After Elsie moved out, a caretaker witnessed the female spirit in the brown dress. A Huguenot Historical Society member sighted a long skirt whoosh around a corner; she raced to identify the person in the house but she found no one.

"Ghosts are former humans with unfinished business on earth."
—David J. Pitkin

Jean Hasbrouck House

Another presence prevails in the 1721 Jean Hasbrouck House. Elizabeth Hasbrouck resided in the house until 1927 and many feel she still inhabits the space albeit in spiritual form. *Someone* remains in the attic... as two boys touring the house inspected the hand-hewn beams, they witnessed a spinning wheel moving forward and backward as if someone sat at the device working wool into yarn. Perhaps Elizabeth is the phantom spinner.

Deyo House

The Deyo House is reported to be haunted by the spirit of 20-year-old expectant mother, Gertrude Deyo, who died of tuberculosis around 1840. The young woman's portrait hangs in the house and a lot of paranormal activity surrounds the painting.

During renovations, curators moved the portraits of Gertrude's parents to the first floor while leaving Gertrude's painting behind on the second floor. That's when the strange happenings began. The portrait fell to the floor and surfaced in different rooms.

Curators took the hint and brought the portrait downstairs to reunite Gertrude's portrait with those of her parents. The action appeased Gertrude's spirit because the paranormal activity surrounding the painting ended.

When the house is empty, docents hear heavy footsteps ascending the servants' staircase. One volunteer even sighted a ghostly woman ascending the staircase and another observed a ghost walk into one of the bedrooms. The worker raced to see who went into the room and found it empty!

LeFevre House

To many who resided in the stone houses, co-habiting with spirits became part and parcel of living in a centuries-old home.

Adjacent to the Old French Church graveyard with its ancient, weathered tombstones is the LeFevre House. Mr. Heidgerd inhabited the house in the early 1900s. During his tenancy, he readily identified the disembodied voices of those he knew and he claimed a steady stream of spirits populated the home including the ghost of a young child.

Author David Pitkin wrote Heidgerd recognized the spirits of husband and wife Margaret Schoonmaker and Daniel Hasbrouck walking about the kitchen. The couple was interred in the cemetery closest to the house so why wouldn't they drop in for a visit?

Huntington Memorial Library

———

62 Chestnut Street
Oneonta

———

Huntington Memorial Library is the former home of Harriet Huntington, mother of Henry Huntington, who donated the land and his ancestral property to the City of Oneonta. Marie Bruni, clairvoyant and the library's retired director, sensed Harriet's presence the day she interviewed with the library.

Marie is gifted with clairvoyance, the ability to gain information about a person, place or thing through means other than the known human senses; it is a form of extra-sensory perception. She witnessed the library's resident spirit nearly every day for decades.

Solon and Harriet Huntington once resided in the Victorian structure. When the prominent couple passed away, their son Henry inherited the property and later bequeathed the house to the city. He asked in return for the library to be renamed "The Huntington Memorial Library" in honor of his parents. The resplendent building still holds many Huntington possessions, including family portraits adorning the walls along the stairwell. Some say Henry's eyes follow their every move, but the genuine ghost here is Harriet — no doubt about it.

Marie's sensitivity to the spirits of the dead gives a rare insight into their personalities and the reasons why they stay behind. In Harriet's case, her reason for lingering is the woman simply loves her house and doesn't want to leave. Oddly though, her spirit did take leave once and stayed away for two years. Marie doesn't know why she left or where Harriet existed in the meantime, but her spirit returned.

Harriet's feelings run the gamut of emotions. Initially sad over the building's disrepair she'll get upset when the place is refurbished. Like most mortals, Harriet doesn't care for change and she shows her displeasure.

Her spirit will act out by taking things and moving them, a mischievous practice that confounds the staff. Once an expensive library catalog went missing for days but finally surfaced in plain sight standing open atop a file cabinet. Although happy with the environment, Harriet's mischief is her way of reminding everyone from time to time that the library is primarily her home.

The library director's office occupies a former servant's bedroom. One time when Marie returned to work after the death of a close friend, Marie discovered a blackbird in her office. The office remained locked during her absence; no way could the bird gain entry. The absence of bird droppings furthered the mystery.

Symbolically birds represent the spirits of the dead. This is one instance that Marie finds unexplainable. The blackbird simply flew away when she opened the window.

Over the years, even patrons witnessed Harriet's translucent apparition and, although startling, they gladly accept the presence of the benevolent ghost.

Oneonta History Center

183 Main Street
Oneonta

The Greater Oneonta Historical Society's History Center is located in the downtown Oneonta Historic District. The Bissell Block, the oldest commercial brick building on Main Street, accommodates the center. Built in 1866, the building housed a hardware store and also served as a restaurant/confectionary and ice cream parlor, dress shop and jewelry store. Today's visitors can enjoy exhibits reflecting Oneonta's rich heritage.

In 1919, John Laskaris purchased Brown's Hardware to relocate his ice cream parlor from across the street. In order to expand his business, he went on to convert the space into a restaurant and candy store. Laskaris' Luncheonette and Confectionary remained a favorite gathering place until 1948.

According to Mark Simonson, the City of the Hills historian, a tragedy occurred in the building over a century ago when a teenage boy accidentally died in the elevator shaft. The historian claims the boy's spirit still lingers in the basement.

Occasionally, when someone dies suddenly, the soul can be confused and not accept the fact they are dead. With unexpected death arises "unfinished business" and the spirit can get stuck between our earthly dimension and the spirit world. These earthbound beings have yet to properly pass over and remain behind accounting for many ghost sightings and haunted places.

Extrasensory perception (ESP) refers to the ability to receive information directly with the mind rather than through the five senses of sight, smell, touch, taste, and hearing. ESP is sometimes called by other names, such as sixth sense, gut feeling, and a hunch. We all possess ESP but the ability manifests differently in each individual.

Marie Bruni, former Huntington Memorial Library Director, possesses an extraordinary sixth sense—she's more "tuned in" than others. She receives images and messages by utilizing her third eye. The third eye (also called the mind's eye or inner eye) is a mystical concept of an invisible eye providing perception beyond ordinary sight.

Bruni's ability enabled her to perceive the boy's presence and she senses the young man doesn't realize he's dead. She says the teenager is a lively spirit and he thinks he's still a flesh and blood energetic youth. A lot of ghosts are confused; they may think they are still alive, or they simply don't want to be dead.

The young man continues to live out his life in a realm where time is measured differently than in our dimension. Even though the boy died decades ago, to him it's a mere moment in time. His spirit stays behind because he is oblivious to the reality of having passed on from the mortal realm and remains in an in-between state.

Phoenicia Library

48 Main Street
Phoenicia

Menacing mansions and creepy castles usually spring to mind when we think of haunted places. But paranormal phenomena can surface in sunny structures as well as in crumbling citadels.

Haunted libraries usually fall into two categories… First, there is the reputedly haunted building where a murder, or other tragedy occurred. The library staff can blame odd noises, books falling off shelves, or computer glitches on the resident ghost.

Second, there are libraries where credible, sensible people observe apparitions, hear disembodied voices, and witness other paranormal events. Staffers learn to live with its resident wraith and accept the paranormal as a normal working condition.

The Phoenicia Library fits both categories. The cheerful yellow structure on Main Street possesses a somewhat eerie history and trustworthy patrons sight a spectacular specter among its stacks.

In the 1880s, the Phoenicia Library building housed a pharmacy and from 1902–1947, a funeral home operated on the premises.

Author David J. Pitkin first presented the story of the Phoenicia Library spirit in *Ghosts of the Northeast*. In 2005, a patron climbed the stairs to use the restroom on the second floor. As he reached his destination, he sighted a gentleman exit the bathroom, tip his hat to the patron and disappear.

Subsequent to the sighting, the library called in a paranormal research team to investigate further. The East Coast Paranormal Investigation Team captured an anomaly on video which, according to the crew, shows "an orb change into a girl and walk out of view and another spirit come into view." The video can be viewed online here: https://www.youtube.com/watch?v=8xAY0HeTLF0.

The team's equipment also registered a temperature drop in the area where the ghost appeared. During the group's investigation, some of their equipment malfunctioned or didn't operate at all because the (brand new) batteries were drained of their energy.

One day, another library customer patiently waited at the counter to borrow books. As she regarded the gentleman seated on the swivel chair behind the counter, she wondered why he sat oblivious to her needing assistance. Suddenly he vanished before her eyes!

Upon opening in the mornings, librarians find incidental items moved from the places they left them the night before. Inexplicably, books fall from library shelves on their own.

A lot of the ghostly activity transpires upstairs. Among the anomalies are the sound of footsteps ascending the stairs, computer glitches and the appearance of sudden cold spots.

Some people love libraries so much, they never leave.

Dodge Inn Restaurant

227 Lake Louise Marie Road
Rock Hill

The Dodge Inn Restaurant originated as a summer boarding house for those seeking fresh air, home cooking and evening entertainment via a record player. In the 1920s, Charlie Porpora purchased the inn with his life savings. Before long, the business operated by Charlie and his wife Margie established a reputation for great lodging and good food. The steak house offered basic fare. Actually, for the first 47 years, no printed menu existed.

Still a wilderness area in the 1920s and 30s, and within driving distance of NYC, the remote inn attracted associates of organized crime. Al Capone became a regular who Charlie's nephew, Frank Porpora, Jr. used to call "Uncle Al." Allegedly, Capone flew in on a pontoon plane and landed on Lake Louise Marie. During this era, farmers, hoteliers, and other Catskill entrepreneurs creatively evaded local and federal authorities in order to provide illegal booze to their clientele. Some say the spirits of long-dead mobsters continue to roam the environs…

Upon his return from World War II, Frank Porpora, Sr. went to work at the restaurant and took over the management in 1948. The Dodge Inn's reputation continued to grow and the eatery became a favorite among locals and the celebrities who entertained Catskills' visitors. Tony Bennett, Milton Berle, Red Buttons, Sid Caesar, Perry Como, Marlene Dietrich, Alan King, Don Rickles, Steve Lawrence, and Eydie Gormé, and boxers Rocky Marciano and Michael Spinks are a few of the superstars who found refuge and a relaxing meal at the restaurant.

During his oversight from 1981–1993, Frank Porpora, Jr. alleged spirits regularly haunted the restaurant. The inexplicable activity occurred in the kitchen such as glasses flying off shelves, pots and pans fell off their hooks and sometimes the water faucets wouldn't turn off. Doors closed at night appeared open in the morning and sometimes motion detectors blared without cause.

One spirit often manifested as a beam of red light and shadowy figures sauntered through the dining room when the place quieted for the night. Were these forms past patrons still enjoying a night out? A spectral cowboy once appeared sitting in the restaurant's "Mafia Room." Perhaps this apparition is a revenant from a nearby dude ranch? Once psychic identified a mustachioed, six-foot tall entity as the spirit of a bounty hunter. He vanished into thin air when a waitress approached him.

Some say a woman's son drowned in the lake while she patronized the inn. A few felt her spirit haunted the inn.

1850 House Hotel

435 Main Street
Rosendale

F irst settled circa 1700, Rosendale received its name from the old "Rosendale Farm" where an inn operated in 1711.

With the discovery of limestone in 1825, the Rosendale natural cement industry commenced during the construction of the Delaware and Hudson Canal. The town prospered as Rosendale cement gained a reputation for quality among engineers. Used in the construction of many U. S. landmarks, including the Brooklyn Bridge, the pedestal of the Statue of Liberty, Federal Hill National Memorial, and one of the wings of the United States Capitol.

As Rosendale flourished, Main Street exploded with businesses to meet every need. Originally known as the Central Hotel, the three-story, red brick building served as a hostelry under a variety of names and hosted countless guests over the decades.

During the 2010 Rosendale Street Festival, the crew filming *Peace, Love & Misunderstanding*, starring Jane Fonda, Catherine Keener, and Elizabeth Olsen, used the building as a staging area.

A sense of the past comes alive in the 1850 building in both physical and abstract ways as the spirits who linger provoke a remembrance of the hotel's history.

Patrons can be assured of their comfort because the elusive, haunted activity is centered in the basement according to staffers. The dimly lit, stone-walled storage room is lined with shelves to hold serveware. Occasionally objects, such as platters and bowls, go missing and reappear in unexpected places.

When psychic medium Bill Wiand explored the hotel's basement he felt an unease; wait staff frequently report discomforting feelings in the area as well as the sound of disembodied footsteps.

Former proprietor Sue Dorsey Morganstern told *Ulster Magazine* that when she owned the hotel with her husband, staffers sighted "miners' legs" walking in the basement.

Dead Man's Stretch

The Rosendale trestle, a 940-foot truss bridge, is part of the defunct Wallkill Valley Railroad. Originally constructed to continue the rail line from New Paltz to Kingston, the bridge rises 150 feet above Rondout Creek.

The trestle opened to rail traffic on April 6, 1872, as the highest span bridge in the United States. Difficult to construct, the truss bridge was a remarkable feat of engineering for its time.

The Rondout Creek beneath the trestle swirls with treacherous currents. Over the years, people jumped, been pushed or fallen into the dangerous waters. In fact, so many perished here, the area became known as "Dead Man's Stretch." The location overflows with reports of ghostly sightings, particularly the apparition of a white dog.

Hardenbergh Manor

NY Route 23
Roxbury

Private Residence

The Hardenbergh Manor stands on land acquired by Johannes Hardenbergh in 1706, and confirmed by Queen Anne's letters patent in 1708. The 1.5 million acre tract, which included the majority of the Catskill Mountain region, became the most important and largest land transaction in colonial history.

Originally part of the Great Hardenbergh Patent, the manor house sits on over an acre of property. Built in 1790 by Johannes, the property is situated at the confluence of the Bear Kill and the Schoharie Creek and is comprised of the main stone home, horse and carriage barn, and a dairy barn. It is the last early stone house built in the village.

Hardenbergh purchased slaves as early as 1792 and became the largest slave owner in New York State. He also established one of the earliest mills in the region, maintained the area's first store, and helped establish the Town of Roxbury in 1799 where he served as the town's first supervisor until 1806.

Multiple paranormal happenings occur in and around the home, most notably involving a window refusing to stay shut. The legendary haunting involves a female slave standing in the window of the manor's top floor, watching Hardenbergh's children playing outside. As she observed the children, she also noticed a party of Native Americans approaching the grounds. She watched as they approached, frantically deciding to alert the children and risk exposing herself. Quickly, she threw open the window and screamed out to the children, but to no avail.

Witnesses discerned a sense of anxiety and observed windows opening on their own. The slave's ghost is often seen in the manor's windows. The particular window that never seems to stay shut is the top floor portal where she watched the children play on that fateful day.

Please note: Hardenbergh Manor is privately owned. Trespassing is strictly prohibited.

Woodchuck Lodge

1633 Burroughs Memorial Road
Roxbury

"These hills fathered and mothered me. I am blood
of their blood and bone of their bone, and why
should I not go back to them in my last years?"
—John Burroughs

Author and naturalist John Burroughs, was born on the family farm near Roxbury. As he worked and played around his rural home, he developed a keen appreciation for nature.

After college, Burroughs moved to Washington D.C. where he worked as a Department of Treasury clerk. He enjoyed writing essays about the beautiful natural surroundings of his far away home. While in Washington, he also became acquainted with the famous poet, Walt Whitman.

Whitman encouraged him to pursue a career in writing. He followed the poet's advice and, in 1867, published his first book, *Notes on Walt Whitman as Poet and Person*, the first published biography of Walt Whitman. Four years later, he published his first collection of essays.

Burroughs is a pioneer in the nature writing genre; over one and a half million copies of his books were sold.

Woodchuck Lodge is a registered National Historic Landmark. The structure served as Burroughs' summer home from 1910 to 1921. Burroughs' older brother Curtis built the lodge in 1862.

The naturalist wrote several essays during his summer sojourns at the lodge and he also entertained luminaries in his home such as Harvey Firestone, Thomas Edison, and Henry Ford.

On his 84th birthday, Burroughs was buried at the foot of a hill, near a large boulder where he used to play as a child and sit to ponder nature as an adult. Those who sit on the rock often experience a cold spot, believed to be the tell-tale sign of Burroughs's spirit presence still occupying the space he loved in life.

Old Stone Fort Museum

145 Fort Road
Schoharie

The Old Stone Fort Museum resides inside a former German High Reform church. Built in 1772, the structure is surrounded by a cemetery, filled with historical artifacts, and haunted by invisible entities.

One of three forts along the Schoharie River, the stockade included blockhouses with mounted cannons. Huts lined the interior walls to shelter local families; the roofs served as a firing step enabling the defenders to shoot over the wall.

In 1780, British troops attacked the building during the Burning of the Valleys. A force of 800 loyalists and Indians under Col. Sir John Johnson and Mohawk Capt. Joseph Brant raided the valley and attacked the fort before proceeding north toward the Mohawk Valley. Cannonball damage is still evident in a corner of the building.

The stockade became obsolete and dismantled in 1785; the building continued as a church until 1844 when the congregation divided and went elsewhere. New York State purchased the property in 1857. Utilized as an armory through the Civil War and until 1873, the state turned it over to Schoharie County for preservation. In 1889, the Schoharie County Historical Society received a charter to operate a museum.

For over 100 years, visitors have learned about the Schoharie Valley's early settlers and their Indian neighbors, viewing artifacts dating to the early 1700s. The second floor exhibits an eclectic collection of antiquities. According to museum director Carle Kopecky, the most common paranormal occurrence experienced here is the sound of incorporeal footsteps coming from the second floor. While locking the building, museum docents heard inexplicable noises upstairs and discerned strange aromas. The spirit activity seem to be associated with the artifacts; spirits could be attached to the objects retaining the energy of those who handled them.

The fort's haunted reputation attracted Syfy Channel's *Ghost Hunters* team to the site. The investigators heard a loud giggle and an invisible someone sit in a chair.

The tower offers views of distant hills and is a favorite surveillance spot for paranormal investigators. The intense energy is palpable and some refuse to go beyond the first few steps leading to a window where a psychic medium observed an ethereal woman looking out toward the cemetery.

The museum offers a program for serious ghost hunters where the paranormal investigators can request a few hours in the building overnight.

Eddy Farm Inn

100 Eddy Farm Road
Sparrow Bush

Once a 100-acre homestead situated on the banks of the Delaware River, the Patterson family named their Eddy Farm after the eddy in the river.

In 1840, the farm catered to raftsmen transporting logs for the shipbuilding industry via the Delaware to Philadelphia. The men easily moored their large timber rafts in Patterson's eddy, one among many along the river.

In the early 1870s, John R. Patterson built Sparrow Bush's first boardinghouse on the farm. Eddy Farm housed summer visitors who sought to escape the oppressive New York City heat.

The operation eventually grew into the historic Eddy Farm Inn and Sports Resort, a 150-room resort hotel on 115 acres offering river bathing, boating, and fishing, tennis, croquet and baseball.

Seven generations of the Patterson family operated the hotel until February 1999, when John and Debra Conway and Steve and Margaret Eisenberg acquired the property.

Comments such as "we don't want to leave," or "we can't wait to come back," are music to innkeeper's ears. At the Eddy Farm, John Conway said a few former guests liked the place so much they never left. Visible only to some, certain guests checked in and never checked out. Visitors often commented they felt a definite energy shift as they approached the historic property.

Many spirits called the lodgings their home. According to some guests, three benevolent ghosts were commonly sighted. Two of the ghosts inhabited the 1907 main building. The other ghost most often manifested in the building known as the "Lodge."

A mysterious specter, elegantly attired in a white gown, appeared in the summer of 1999. Three guests encountered her spirit. She surprised one lodger as he showered. Another met the wraith in the hallway; the white lady brushed past the visitor as she hurried to the staircase. On the main floor, the specter caught the attention of a third witness because he sensed her urgency and observed her odd behavior until she vanished before his eyes.

"...to the great Spirit and Fountain of life, all things, in both space and time, must be present... action once begun never ceases... thus the past is always present, although, for the purpose of fitting us for this mortal life, our ordinary senses are so constituted as to be unperceptive of these phenomena."

—Catherine Crowe, *The Night-Side of Nature*

W.J. LINTON SC.

Acknowledgments

*C*atskill Ghosts originated as a labor of love and expanded into an exciting learning experience! Throughout the process, I spoke to the most genial and interesting individuals who provided a wealth of eerie and historic information, and in some cases, photographs.

I'd like to convey my deepest gratitude to Trish Bergan, Director, Dr. Best House & Medical Museum; Marie Bruni, Director (retired), Huntington Memorial Library, Oneonta; Robert Brzozowski, President, Oneonta Historical Society; John Conway, Sullivan County Historian; Edwin Ford, Kingston Historian; Sam Lewit, former Wildmere Hotel staffer, Lake Minnewaska; Barbara O'Rourke, Co-founder, Sullivan Paranormal Society, Sullivan County; Sara Ottaviano, Highland Public Library; Gary Robusto, Founder, Tri-City NY Paranormal Society, Albany; and Mark Simonson, Historian, City of Oneonta.

Special recognition is owed to the late David J. Pitken for his in-depth, spirit-filled books.

I am grateful to Maryann Way for her invaluable guidance.

In appreciation to Tina Kush Crepezzi for proofreading the manuscript.

As ever, thank you Deb Tremper, Graphic Designer, Six Penny Graphics for *Catskill Ghosts'* cover design and interior layout.

Many, many thanks to the booksellers who market my books.

Most of all, thank YOU for reading!

"There is much hope expressed in ghost tales, for it seems certain that the most vital part of our being does survive the end of our body's functioning. So, death is not only not an end, it cannot be ... "

—*David J. Pitkin*

Bibliography

Chowdhury, Partha P. "Supernatural elements in Washington Irving's Rip Van Winkle." http://tapashiba.blogspot.com/2016/06/supernatural-elements-in-washington.html.

Conway, John. "A Halloween Ghost Story." *Times Herald-Record,* October 26, 2012.

_____. "The Ghost of Laura Darling Kahl." *Times Herald-Record,* October 31, 2014.

Drollinger, Linda. "Weird and Wild Kenoza Lake." *The River Reporter,* August 2, 2017.

Favicchio, Donna. "Valley of the Spirits." *Highland Mid-Hudson Post,* October 28, 2004.

Farnsworth, Cheri. *Haunted Hudson Valley: Ghosts and Strange Phenomena of New York's Sleepy Hollow Country.* Stackpole Books, 2009.

Foderaro, Lisa W. "The Librarians Call It An Anomaly (It Wasn't Rattling Chains)." *New Paltz Journal,* April 20, 2008.

Gibbons, Ann. "New life for Rosendale staple." *The Daily Freeman,* August 26, 2012.

Greenberg, Peter. "Haunted Hotels Rooms with a BOO!" http://www.angelfire.com/ri/spookycat/travelhaunts.html.

Hall-Dukin, Elizabeth. "Spooks of the Catskills." *Catskill Mountain Region Guide,* October 2016.

Hauck, Dennis William. *Haunted Places, The National Directory.* Penguin Books, 1996.

Hawes, Jason. "The Oldest House in Georgia." *Ghost Hunters.* Syfy Channel, Season 6, Episode 20.

_____. "Ghosts of Christmas Past." *Ghost Hunters,* Syfy Channel, Season 6, Episode 24.

_____. "Well of Horror." *Ghost Hunters.* Syfy Channel, Season 7, Episode 17.

_____. "Last Will and Evidence." *Ghost Hunters*. Syfy Channel, Season 10, Episode 3.

Hine, Charles Gilbert. *History and Legend: Fact, Fancy and Romance of the Old Mine Road, Kingston, New York, To the Mine Holes of Pahaquarry*. Hines Annual, 1908.

Hulse, David. "Remembering the Battle at Minisink." *The River Reporter*, July 15–21, 2014.

IBSSG, Julia. "Black Sheep Sunday: Memories of Sally Hamilton's Murder." http://nightbeforenoon.blogspot.com/2009/07/black-sheep-sunday-memories-of-sally.html.

Jones, Louis C., *Things That Go Bump in the Night*. Syracuse University Press, 1983.

La Monica, Lisa. *Haunted Catskills*. The History Press, 2013.

Latterra, Salena. "The Borscht Belt." *The Daily Rant*, November 22, 2005. http://www.salenalettera.com/2005/11/borscht-belt.html.

Levine, David. "History of Borscht Belt Hotels and Bungalow Colonies in the Catskills." *Hudson Valley Magazine*, August 2014.

_____. "A History of Steamboat Racing and Shipwrecks in the Hudson River. *Hudson Valley Magazine*, September 2014.

Lewit, Sam. "Lake Minnewaska Mountain Houses." Summer 2009. http://abouttown.us/articles/lake-minnewaska-mountain-houses.

Lynn, Naomi. "Haunted Hotel Makes You Sign A Waiver Before You Stay." August 12, 2016. http://lite987.com/ny-haunted-hotel-waiver-before-stay.

Macken, Lynda Lee. *Haunted Houses of the Hudson Valley*. Black Cat Press, 2006.

_____. *Ghosts of Central New York*. Black Cat Press, 2009.

_____. *Empire Ghosts, Historic Haunts in New York State*. Black Cat Press, 2018.

Marshall, Jessica Bloustein & Garrett, Patrick. "The Horseman of Leeds." *Listen With The Lights On*, July 10, 2016. http://www.wamc.org/post/podcast-horseman-leeds.

Medenbach, Deborah. "The History Hunters, A psychic tour of Ulster County." *Ulster County Magazine*, September/October 2014.

Middleburgh Library Staff. "The Historic Dr. Best House and Medical Museum." http://www.middleburghlibrary.info/dr-best-house.

Mitchell, Paula. "Chilling Ghost Stories of Old Ulster County Jail Retold. https://hudsonvalleynewsnetwork.com/2017/10/30/chilling-ghost-stories-old-ulster-county-jail-retold.

"Murder in Room 12." *The Haunted*. Animal Planet, Season 2, Episode 26, May 13, 2011.

Nicosia, Patsy. "Middleburgh's Best House, Medical Exhibit one-of-a-kind." *Times-Journal*, April 17, 2018.

Perjatel, Maria. "Exploring the Haunted History Trail of New York State." September 13, 2018. https://magazine.northeast.aaa.com/daily/travel/road-trips/haunted-history-new-york-state.

Pitken, David J. *Ghosts of the Northeast*. Aurora Publications, 2002.

_____. *New York State Ghosts, Volume 1*. Aurora Publications, 2006.

_____. *New York State Ghosts, Volume Two*. Aurora Publications, 2008.

Schneider, Caitlin. "The Long, Haunted History of New York's Shanley Hotel." August 12, 2016. http://mentalfloss.com/article/84568/long-haunted-history-new-yorks-shanley-hotel.

"Shawangunk Country Club." *Wawarsing.Net Magazine*. Issue 7, June 2003.

Silverman, Stephen M. & Silver, Raphael D. *The Catskills, Its History and How It Changed America*. Alfred A. Knopf, 2015.

Sullivan County Historical Society. "The Stone Arch Bridge." November 3, 2011. http://www.scnyhistory.org/index.php/history/delaware/50-history/cochecton/458-the-stone-arch-bridge.

The Haunting Of Meat Loaf. Lifetime Network. Season 4, Episode 7, 2015.

"Top Model Falls from Tree to Her Death near Woodstock." *Schenectady Gazette*, September 9, 1969.

Tymn, Michael. "Trying to make Sense of Ghosts." January 13, 2014. http://whitecrowbooks.com/michaeltymn/entry/trying_to_make_sense_of_ghosts.

Vedder, J. Van Vechten. *Historic Catskill*. Catskill, 1922.

Werner, James W. jwwerner.com/ODC/OldDutchChurch.html.

Whitman, Victor. "Owners dodge ghosts at spooky Sullivan County eatery." *Times Herald–Record*, October 30, 2006.

WSKG Public Media. "Haunted History, the Frisbee House." October 2, 2014. https://www.youtube.com/watch?v=rEUNYLrrf2A.

Zimmermann, Linda. *Ghost Investigator, Volume 7, Psychic Impressions*. Eagle Press, 2007.

_____. *Ghost Investigator, Volume 8, Back into the Light*. Spirited Books, 2008.

_____. *Hudson Valley Haunts*. Schiffer Publishing, 2009.

PHOTO CREDITS:

WEBSITES:

Burn Brae Mansion: http://www.burnbraemansion.com

The Catskills Institute: https://catskillsinstitute.northeastern.edu

Delaware & Hudson Canal Museum:
http://www.canalmuseum.org/depuy-canal-house

Delaware County Historical Association: http://www.dcha-ny.org

CATSKILL GHOSTS

Depuy Canal House: http://www.depuycanalhouse.com/history

Dr. Best House & Medical Exhibit: https://www.drbesthouse.com

Elting Memorial Library: http://www.eltinglibrary.org

Ethelbert B. Crawford Public Library: https://ebcpl.org

Great Northern Catskills: https://www.greatnortherncatskills.com

Haunted History Trail of New York State: https://hauntedhistorytrail.com

Hudson River Maritime Museum:
http://www.hrmm.org/rondout-lighthouse.html

Lake Minnewaska: http://www.lakeminnewaska.org

Listen With The Lights On: http://www.wamc.org/programs/listen-lights

National Park Service: https://www.nps.gov/nr/travel/kingston/k4.htm

The Old Stone Fort Museum: https://theoldstonefort.org

Shadowland Stages: https://shadowlandstages.org

Shanley Hotel: https://thehauntedshanleyhotel.com

Shawangunk Country Club: http://www.shawangunkcountryclub.com

The Stewart House: http://www.stewarthouse.com/

Sullivan Paranormal Society:
http://sullivanparanormal.wixsite.com/sullivanparanormalsociety

Thomas Cole National Historic Site: https://thomascole.org

Tri-City NY Paranormal Society:
https://www.tri-citynyparanormalsociety.com

Wikipedia: https://www.wikipedia.org

Woodchuck Lodge: http://jbwoodchucklodge.org

Other Titles
by Lynda Lee Macken

Adirondack Ghosts
Adirondack Ghosts II
Adirondack Ghosts III
Array of Hope, An Afterlife Journal
Empire Ghosts, Historic Haunts in New York State
Ghost Hunting the Mohawk Valley
Ghostly Gotham, Haunted History of New York City
*Ghosts of Central New York
Ghosts of the Garden State
Ghosts of the Garden State II
Ghosts of the Garden State III
Ghosts of the Jersey Shore
Ghosts of the Jersey Shore II
Haunted Baltimore
Haunted Cape May
Haunted History of Staten Island
Haunted Houses of New Jersey
Haunted Houses of the Hudson Valley
Haunted Lake George
Haunted Lake Placid
Haunted Long Beach Island
Haunted Long Island
Haunted Long Island II
Haunted Monmouth County
Haunted New Hope
Haunted Salem & Beyond

*(originally published as *Leatherstocking Ghosts*)

Enjoy Lynda Lee Macken's Adirondack series of haunting tales...

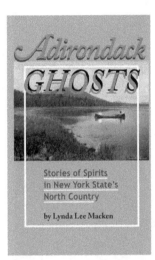

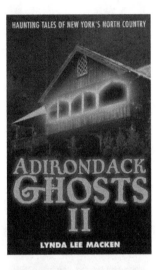

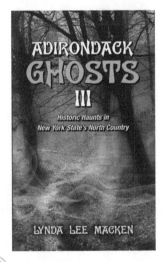

Available wherever books are sold.

CPSIA information can be obtained
at www.ICGtesting.com
Printed in the USA
FSHW012309120619
59006FS

9 780982 958094